Teaching
as
Principled
Practice

We dedicate this book
to the children in the Oakland Public Schools
who deserve the best education and the best teachers.

Teaching as Principled Practice

Managing Complexity for Social Justice

Linda R. Kroll • Ruth Cossey • David M. Donahue
Tomás Galguera • Vicki Kubler LaBoskey
Anna Ershler Richert • Philip Tucher

Mills College

SAGE Publications
Thousand Oaks • London • New Delhi

For information:

 Sage Publications, Inc.
2455 Teller Road
Thousand Oaks, California 91320
E-mail: order@sagepub.com

Sage Publications Ltd.
1 Oliver's Yard
55 City Road
London EC1Y 1SP
United Kingdom

Sage Publications India Pvt. Ltd.
B-42, Panchsheel Enclave
Post Box 4109
New Delhi 110 017 India

Printed in the United States of America

Library of Congress Cataloging-in-Publication Data

Teaching as principled practice: Managing complexity for social justice / by Linda R. Kroll . . . [et al.].
    p. cm.
Includes bibliographical references and index.
ISBN 0-7619-2875-8 (cloth)—ISBN 0-7619-2876-6 (pbk.)
    1. Teachers—Training of—United States. 2. Educational sociology—United States. 3. Social justice—Study and teaching—United States. I. Kroll, Linda Ruth.
LB1715.T428 2005
370'.71'1—dc22   2004003261

04 05 06 07 10 9 8 7 6 5 4 3 2 1

Acquisitions Editor:	Diane McDaniel
Editorial Assistant:	Margo Beth Crouppen
Production Editor:	Melanie Birdsall
Copy Editor:	Jackie Tasch
Typesetter:	C&M Digitals (P) Ltd.
Proofreader:	Mary Meagher
Indexer:	Kathy Paparchontis
Cover Designer:	Janet Foulger

Contents

Acknowledgments

This book owes its inspiration to the enthusiasm, hard work, thoughtful questioning, and dedication to social justice of the graduate students in the Teachers for Tomorrow's Schools Teacher Education Program at Mills College. They, along with their cooperating teachers and supervisors, help us to teach in ways that will prepare these novice teachers for urban schools as they are now and as they could be. The graduate students helped us to confront the knotty problems that besiege them regularly in their public school classrooms and to think with them about ways to understand and solve these problems. To all of them—students, cooperating teachers, and supervisors—thank you.

Likewise, we could never have finished this book without the support and care from the people at Sage Publishing who have seen us through the whole process: Todd Armstrong, who helped us get started and helped us to find the audience to whom we wanted to speak; Diane McDaniel, who provided thoughtful comments and guidance with regard to content and voice; Margo Crouppen, who answered every question at least twice and guided us through all the editorial and manuscript details. Sage also provided us with a wonderful set of reviewers, whose positive comments and suggestions helped us make necessary refinements and clarifications.

Early on in the conception of this book, Miriam Ben-Peretz and Pamela Grossman, in their roles as discussants at the American Educational Research Association (AERA) helped us question and clarify what it was that we meant by principles of practice.

Finally, our families and friends have supported us in the writing of this text. They understand the importance of social justice and excellent outcomes for all children and youth and, in innumerable ways, help us to do our work.

Preface

Linda R. Kroll

You are about to embark on a reading journey that will introduce you to a conception about teaching and learning to teach that may differ from any you have previously considered. While we believe that many of this book's ideas can be applied in a variety of settings, we also know that context is an essential part of the picture. Thus, we want to take this opportunity to introduce our contexts and ourselves.

All of the authors of this book teach in the Education Department at Mills College in Oakland, California, a highly diverse urban community in the San Francisco Bay Area. Mills has had a long and persistent commitment to the preparation of teachers. Members of our department have been involved in local, state, national, and international conversations about teacher education since the early 20th century. The department houses the oldest laboratory school on the West Coast (established in 1926), teaching children between the ages of 3 months and 10 years old. The department provides graduate programs in teacher education, educational leadership, and early childhood care and education.

Mills is located in an urban setting where the public schools have had great difficulty in providing adequately for the students in the community. The department is committed to contributing to the development of excellent teachers for such urban settings. In addition, the department is dedicated to providing educational leaders for urban schools, professionals who will serve the needs of young children in preschools, child care, and hospitals and act as advocates for their well-being. Like many other institutions, we continue to struggle with the dilemmas of providing excellent educational opportunities for all children in urban settings. Although we have yet to "figure it out," we are devoted to an agenda of social justice, equitable opportunities, and excellent outcomes for children and youth in the public schools.

For many years, the Department of Education has been working with a vision for effective urban education. We began with three big ideas: inquiry and reflective practice as essential to good teaching, a knowledge of developmental theory as a way of understanding how people learn, and a determination that the teachers we prepared would be agents of change in the schools. As new members have joined our team, our vision of social justice, equity, and excellent outcomes for all children has been refined and clarified. New ideas have replaced earlier ones, and our conceptions about what good teaching is and how we might proceed with preparing teachers to do this important work have grown and changed over time as well.

Currently, our program is guided by the six principles we write about in this book. These principles reflect our best thinking about the purposes of teaching and public school education. They guide us in both what and how we teach. While these principles are constantly under consideration and review, they serve as a touchstone for us as we engage in our challenging and changing work. The principles are:

- Teaching is a moral act founded on an ethic of care.
- Teaching is an act of inquiry and reflection.
- Learning is a constructivist/developmental process.
- The acquisition of subject matter and content knowledge is essential.
- Teaching is a collegial act and requires collaboration.
- Teaching is essentially a political act.

As a composite, the principles provide a set of lenses that help us to understand our practice. They also help us focus toward a shared goal as we strive to help teachers learn to create classrooms in which social justice, equity, and powerful learning occur.

The Mills College Teacher for Tomorrow's Schools program is a two-year program with a cohort of 60 students each year. The program is divided into four subgroups: a middle and secondary school program in mathematics and science, a middle and secondary school program in English and social studies, an elementary school program, and an elementary school program with an emphasis in early childhood education. Most courses in the program are taught by the seven faculty who are the authors of this book. Faculty also supervise student teachers in their placements, as do a number of part-time faculty. Many part-time faculty are graduates of the program. Hence, the faculty is very cohesive in its understanding and agreement about the principles. They have lived them as both students and teachers. We find this cohesion contributes to a passionate sense of purpose and strong collegiality among the group, while we remain alert to the possible limitations of insularity. Although we have a unified vision, we do not all agree about everything. This diversity of understandings and beliefs makes for lively discussions and a much broader worldview than might otherwise be so.

In writing this book, each of us began by taking one principle to research and elaborate. We have presented this work at several research conferences where our goal was to demonstrate how the principles helped us teach preservice teachers to become effective teachers in urban schools (Galguera, 1998a, 1998b; Kroll, 1998a, 1998b; LaBoskey, 1998a, 1998b; Richert, 1998a, 1998b). From these presentations came the inspiration to write a book about what we do and what we believe is an effective way to think about teaching as principled practice and a lifelong learning process. Each of us is primarily responsible for one chapter where we discuss one principle. Thus, when we write about that principle, the examples we use are from our own particular teaching experiences. It is important to understand, however, that any of us could have written any of the chapters.

The process of writing this book allowed us a wonderful opportunity to practice most of the principles ourselves. We believe strongly in the moral and political significance of the work we do, and this collaboration gave us a chance to go public with our beliefs. In writing, we constantly had to reflect and inquire into our own practices to see how they represented principled practice. In thinking about the purpose of the book, we had to consider for whom we were writing and how they would best understand our message, thus taking into account both the nature of learning and development and the subject matter (learning to teach) that we are considering. Last, and perhaps most significant, this process has afforded us an incredible opportunity for collegial collaboration. In working together, we have learned so much about what it is we want to do and what we strive to do. In addition, we have learned about each other. The end result for us as a faculty is a stronger working relationship filled with admiration and respect for one another. We know how lucky we are to be working together. We hope, as you read this book, you will join us in deliberating about the usefulness of principled practice in teaching and learning to teach.

What follows are brief professional biographies for each of the authors, so that you can know the context from which we come and from which we each personally speak.

Ruth Cossey, Ph.D., Associate Professor and Codirector of the Mid-Career Mathematics and Science Teacher Credential program at Mills College, has 10 years of experience teaching preservice teacher candidates in Oakland. She has also taught mathematics in urban public schools for nine years. She served as a senior mathematics educator with EQUALS and FAMILY MATH at the Lawrence Hall of Science at the University of California, Berkeley, for 10 years. Dr. Cossey has for the past two years been principal investigator and director of *Algebra: What Works?* (AWW), funded by the University of California. Central to her work has been the importance of classroom mathematical discourse to deepening students' understandings and abilities to communicate those understandings. An extended sample of her skill as a mathematics educator has been captured in the 2001 "Learning Math: Patterns, Functions and Algebra," a videotaped professional development course in mathematics produced by Annenberg/CPB Channel with the Harvard Smithsonian Center for Astrophysics.

David M. Donahue, Ph.D., is Assistant Professor of Education at Mills College, Oakland, where he is also Codirector of the secondary English-social studies teacher credential program. Previously, he was a curriculum writer and developmental editor and social studies teacher in public schools. He has worked with Amnesty International's Human Rights Education program and the Canadian Human Rights Foundation over the past 10 years and has developed and led training programs on human rights for teachers and activists in the United States, Eastern Europe, and Central Asia. He is the author of two human rights curriculum guides, *Lesbian, Gay, Bisexual, and Transgender Rights: A Human Rights Perspective* and, with Nancy Flowers, *The Uprooted: Refugees and the United States*. His research interests include learning from community service and preparing secondary teachers to teach reading and writing in subject area classes.

Tomás Galguera, Ph.D., is Associate Professor of Education at Mills College, Oakland, where he codirects the pre-K-elementary Early Childhood Emphasis and Developmental Perspectives in Teaching teacher credential program. He specializes in English language-development methodology courses for both elementary and secondary preservice teachers and has been a certified Spanish-bilingual elementary public school teacher in Oakland. In addition to contributing to the *Full Options Science System's Newsletter* and publishing in *The Multilingual Educator,* he developed high school science curriculum modules for teachers of English learners and was a contributing author of *Professional Development for Teachers of English Learners: A Scaffold for Change,* published by the San Diego County Office of Education. Together with Joshua Fishman, he published *Introduction to Test Construction in the Social and Behavioral Sciences* and, with Kenji Hakuta, is a contributing author to *Psychology and Educational Practice,* edited by Herbert J. Walberg and Geneva D. Haertel. His research interests include the pedagogy of teacher preparation for language-minority students and exploration of ethnicity, race, culture, and language in education.

Linda R. Kroll, Ph.D., is Professor in the Department of Education at Mills College. She has taught at Mills since 1988 and served for two years as Dean and Chair of the department. She codirects the early childhood portion of the Teachers for Tomorrow's Schools Program, known as Developmental Perspectives in Teaching. Her research interests focus on applying developmental and constructivist theory to understanding and facilitating children's and teachers' learning. She has been a preschool teacher for emotionally disturbed children and an elementary school teacher in Vallejo, California, where she taught combined classes of kindergarteners through third graders for nine years. She has been a teacher educator since 1979, and she helped found the UC Berkeley Developmental Teacher Education Program. Her work with children focused on urban settings for children with special needs, English language learners, and children of color, who are traditionally underserved. Her work with teachers has focused on urban school settings and the Mills College Laboratory School. She is a contributing author to *Reframing Teacher Education: Dimensions of a Constructivist Approach,* edited by Julie Rainer, and *How Students Learn: Reforming Schools Through Learner-Centered Education,* edited by Nadine Lambert and Barbara McCombs. She is currently president of the Association for Constructivist Teaching.

Vicki Kubler LaBoskey, Ph.D., is Professor of Education at Mills College, Oakland, where she is also Director of the elementary teacher credential program. Previously, she was an urban elementary school teacher in East Los Angeles and San Jose, California, where she taught multiethnic classes of kindergarteners through fourth graders for eight years. She has been a teacher educator since 1985; she was the associate director of the Stanford Teacher Education Program for three years before coming to Mills. She is currently president-elect of the California Council on Teacher Education and chair of the Self-Study of Teacher Education Practices Special Interest Group of the American Educational Research Association. Her most recent publications include *Narrative Inquiry in Practice: Advancing the Knowledge of Teaching*, with Nona Lyons, and the two-volume *International Handbook of Self-Study of Teaching and Teacher Education Practice*, with John Loughran, Mary Lynn Hamilton, and Tom Russell. Her research interests focus on the self-study of teacher education practices and on narrative approaches to the development and mentoring of critical reflection and inquiry in teaching.

Anna Ershler Richert, Ph.D., is Professor of Education at Mills College where she codirects the Teachers for Tomorrow's Schools Credential Program. She came to Mills from Stanford University, where she was associate director of the Stanford Teacher Education Program for three years. She is active in various school reform efforts both locally and nationally, including the Coalition of Essential Schools and Bay Area School Reform Collaborative. Currently, she is a teacher education scholar with the Carnegie Foundation for the Advancement of Teaching and Learning and secretary of Division K of the AERA. Recent publications reflect her interest in narrative methodology for teacher education and teacher research. They include two book chapters: "Narratives That Teach: Learning About Teaching From the Stories Teachers Tell," in *Narrative Knowing in Teaching: Exemplars of Reflective Teaching, Research and Teacher Education*, Nona Lyons and Vicki LaBoskey, editors; and "Narratives as Experience Texts: Writing Themselves Back In," in *Teachers Caught in the Action: The Work of Professional Development*, A. Lieberman and L. Miller, editors. Her research interests focus on teacher inquiry, teacher professional development, and the pedagogy of teacher education.

Philip Tucher, M.A., is a Visiting Assistant Professor of Education at Mills College, Oakland, where he directs the Teacher Institute for Urban Fieldwork, a forum for teacher mentors focused on issues of equitable and excellent outcomes for students in urban classrooms. He is codirector of the Mid-Career Mathematics and Science Program for secondary credential candidates. He teaches math and science methods courses and specializes in fostering collaborative interaction and placing mathematical and scientific reasoning at the heart of classroom practice. For the past 10 years, he has worked with teachers in several parts of the United States to improve student achievement by raising the quality and levels of academic interaction that takes place when students are working in small groups in heterogeneous classrooms. He is interested in the use of lesson study in teacher preparation. Before coming to Mills, Tucher was assistant principal at a middle school in the San Lorenzo Unified School District in the Bay Area.

❖ REFERENCES

Galguera, T. (1998a, April). Teaching is a political act. In W. Ayers (chair), *Principled practice in teacher education: An interactive symposium,* presented at the annual meeting of the American Educational Research Association, San Diego, CA.

Galguera, T. (1998b, October). Teaching is a political act. In L. R. Kroll (chair), *Principled practice in teacher education: An interactive symposium,* presented at the annual meeting of the Association for Constructivist Teaching, Oakland, CA.

Kroll, L. R. (1998a, April). Constructivism in teacher education. In W. Ayers (chair), *Principled practice in teacher education: An interactive symposium,* presented at the annual meeting of the American Educational Research Association, San Diego, CA.

Kroll, L. R. (1998b, October). Constructivism in teacher education. In L. R. Kroll (chair), *Principled practice in teacher education: An interactive symposium,* presented at the annual meeting of the Association for Constructivist Teaching, Oakland, CA.

LaBoskey, V. K. (1998a, April). "Not just a series of fun activities": Preparing to teach content. In W. Ayers (chair), *Principled practice in teacher education: An interactive symposium,* presented at the annual meeting of the American Educational Research Association, San Diego, CA.

LaBoskey, V. K. (1998b, October). "Not just a series of fun activities": Preparing to teach content. In L. R. Kroll (chair), *Principled practice in teacher education: An interactive symposium,* presented at the annual meeting of the Association for Constructivist Teaching, Oakland, CA.

Richert, A. E. (1998a, April). Preparing the moral practitioner. In W. Ayers (chair), *Principled practice in teacher education: An interactive symposium,* presented at the annual meeting of the American Educational Research Association, San Diego, CA.

Richert, A. E. (1998b, October). Preparing the moral practitioner. In L. R. Kroll (chair), *Principled practice in teacher education: An interactive symposium,* presented at the annual meeting of the Association for Constructivist Teaching, Oakland, CA.

Foreword

Rebecca Akin

S andra Cisneros's short story, "Salvador Late or Early," is slightly more than 300 words long, barely filling one printed page of her collection, *Woman Hollering Creek.* More poetry than prose, this piece of writing provides a brief glimpse into the life of Salvador, a "forty pound body of boy" who is perhaps 6 years old. Depending on the audience, one sees Salvador as a hero or a responsible family member, as unfortunate or abused (Campano, 2003). Although she leaves the interpretation to the reader, Cisneros manages, with such brilliance and in so few words, to reveal how this child is framed as invisible through the lens of school:

> Salvador with the eyes the color of caterpillar, Salvador of the crooked hair and crooked teeth, Salvador whose name the teacher cannot remember, is a boy who is no one's friend, runs along somewhere in that vague direction where homes are the color of bad weather, lives behind a raw wood doorway, shakes the sleepy brothers awake, ties their shoes, combs their hair with water, feeds them milk and corn flakes from a tin cup in the dim dark of the morning.
>
> Salvador, late or early, sooner or later arrives with the string of younger brothers ready. (Cisneros, 1992, p. 10)[1]

As a teacher, I've had many students who would find Salvador heroic, recognizing him as their older brother or maybe seeing themselves in him. Over the years, my own interpretation of children I see in Salvador has been complicated. Disruptive late arrivals, inconvenient early arrivals, struggles communicating with families who don't speak English, judgmental silence, frustration with a lack of contact with parents who are working, busy, weary both of me, a middle-class white woman, and the institution of school—all interpretations I unconsciously wrap around children like Salvador, who are seen through my own historical and cultural lenses.

What I hope to illustrate through Cisneros's portrait of Salvador is that, as teachers, we have the power to "story" students in a way that frames their educational experience. Although we are likely to remember their names, we may know nothing about who they are. We may be unfamiliar with their communities and see where they live as a vague place, contrasting simply to that which we do know. Their late and early arrivals reinforce our notions of unreliability, of half-presence. Often without knowing that we are doing so, we interpret what we don't understand as "other" or as invisible, simply because our own life experiences are necessarily limited. To whatever degree each of us struggles to understand our students, the power of the impact we have on children in these interpretive ways lies at the very center of what it means to teach.

In the book that follows here, the authors, themselves teachers, will discuss the ways in which they try to help their students, preservice teachers, begin their process of learning to teach. Their writing is framed in terms of six principles that guide their practice. The principles are focused around justice, equity, care, knowledge, growth, and power; at the core, they honor the welfare of students like Salvador. The voice I write from here in introducing their work is as former student, colleague, first-grade teacher, and cooperating teacher of the students these teacher educators teach.

As a teacher, it has been my experience that knowing students well is the most important, and by far the most difficult, of my responsibilities. It's one thing to think about a student like Salvador through the beauty of Cisneros's language. It's another to encounter him in a classroom, where one's attention is focused on a whirl of subject matter, management issues, assessment, immediate physical needs, standards, and contextual factors; where an actual child, particularly one of Salvador's nature—quiet, unobtrusive, outwardly complacent—can be a mystery who easily slips under the radar screen. As I hope the following narrative excerpt from my own teaching will help illustrate, in even the smallest account of classroom interaction so much of this complexity is revealed:

Working on a lesson from a unit on place value, the class is struggling explicitly for the first time with the distinction between *tens* and *ones*. This work time following our group introduction meets with various levels of success. Iris and Helen can place the digit *1* representing *tens* and *5* representing the *ones* from their solution of *15* in the correct column, but neither can verbally explain to me why, even though the picture they have collaboratively drawn to represent their thinking makes sense.

Michael, who insists on working alone, counts to 18 instead of 15 and then records both digits in the ones column. His drawing shows 14 individual linker cubes, arbitrarily placed around the page. Thomas, his silenced partner, copies his incorrect answer of 18 but draws his cubes in a way that indicates to me he understands the work.

AnLe, who speaks only Cantonese, builds her linker cubes into stairs, yet records her work perfectly on her paper. Mei, who can communicate with both of us, translates an explanation I don't understand. It doesn't help that, as I'm trying to hear her soft voice, an announcement from the office loudly interrupts for the third time today, informing us that the heat should be back on by the afternoon. I spy Karl and Lavon building a fort with their manipulatives.

I'm about to investigate when Salvador arrives, an hour late now, shoes squeaking with water, pants soaked up to his knees from his walk to school in the rain. On my way to help him, I notice Marcus with his head down on the table, quietly sleeping. Later, he'll tell me that he spent the night in the emergency room of the county hospital. With his infant sister and his mother, he took two buses to get there in the middle of the night. He reveals in graphic detail how his mother's arm, which required 10 stitches, bled the whole way.

Although I've substituted *Salvador* for my own student's name to illustrate my point, what unfolds here is one brief moment in a morning that is very typical of my year, one much like those experienced by my Mills graduate colleagues who teach in the urban districts surrounding the campus. As one can see, in the immediacy of the classroom, Salvador himself becomes small—even smaller somehow than his 40-pound body would suggest. What we see in this account is that there is so much going on at every moment for a teacher in her classroom that of necessity she functions in a place firmly situated between the automatic and the intuitive. There is simply too little time to stop and struggle with the many and varied responses required of us throughout the day. To then think of Salvador as Cisneros describes him, "inside that wrinkled shirt, inside that throat that must clear itself and apologize each time it speaks, inside that 40-pound body of boy with its geography of scars, its history of hurt, . . . in that cage of the chest where something throbs with both fists and knows only what Salvador knows" (p. 11), would call forth too much that is at the core of all the dilemmas my Mills colleagues and I face in thinking deeply about schooling. We might find ourselves overwhelmed with emotion (a feeling we often fight) to the point of inaction. Salvador's story is only 1 of 20 in my classroom. When he is in high school, his will be 1 of 150 stories for his teachers. But to not think of him from the perspective Cisneros offers renders him largely invisible. To keep Salvador in one's mind and heart and, at the same time, to teach him and his classmates in the context of the classroom requires a deep, complex, and principled foundation.

It is this complex foundation on which the "automatic" and the "intuitive" mentioned above function. These are not unthinking states, nor are they a reaction to being overwhelmed. They are, in fact, a huge part of what teaching is about—being able to negotiate many different needs in the moment, both anticipated and unexpected, and to do so while holding firmly in view subject matter objectives, developmental expectations, physical and emotional needs, knowledge of individual students, and the implications, both large and small, of our work together.

It is the building of this foundation that is the work written about here by the authors in this book. Each addresses a specific principle that is a core component of the foundation the faculty in the Mills College Teachers for Tomorrow's Schools Program tries to help their students establish, principles addressing the moral and political nature of teaching, inquiry, and collaboration as methodologies, subject matter acquisition as a goal, and learning theory as a foundation on which teaching decisions rest. As readers will note as these chapters unfold, each author writes about a specific principle, but embedded in the writing of each is evidence of the presence of the others. Whether this was their intention, I don't know, but I do know that this is exactly as it should be. As a teacher, I've found that what the authors are referring to here as principles are so interconnected in my mind that rather than individual, bounded ideas (although they are that, too), they come together in practice in a way that one cannot be thought of without consideration of the others.

It is my recollection that these principles were seldom explicitly mentioned when I was a student. Certainly, they were not on a list that we were expected to memorize. We were not assessed on our ability to recite them. What was explicit—in the course work, through the teaching, in our interactions, with the language used, through conversation, in the various texts produced and with which we engaged—was the actual presence of these principles, fully enacted as well as illustrated. The teaching of these authors itself was guided by these principles, so that rather than simply being talked about in their teaching, the principles were lived. The impact of such modeling was extraordinarily powerful. The principles became mine because I was immersed in them, I had to grapple with them; they pushed my thinking and my way of understanding the world until finally I not only understood them, but I understood why they mattered. That I left my years as a student at Mills with these principles internalized is not to say that, as a teacher, I was fully formed, knowing what to do in the complex environment of my classroom, school, district, and community. Uncertainties and insecurities and doubts abounded (and abound still). Instead of a repertoire of formulaic responses or prescriptions for what to do, however, what I developed was a beginning yet firm foundation that itself would continue to grow and deepen over the years—a frame that helped guide my thinking, questions, dilemmas, uncertainties, emotions, doubts, beliefs, learning, decisions, and actions.

Most important to our role as teachers of children, seeing through the lens of these principles has helped me over the years to complicate my understanding both of my students and the place of schooling in their lives. Being able to negotiate the immediacy of the classroom is unimportant if that is not done with a complex and deep understanding and belief in the individuals who make up that classroom. Always to some extent bounded by my own cultural, class, and gendered perspectives, it is necessary that I have the tools that my internalization of these principles provides to help me see beyond what I think I might know about my students to what they might actually be. With that ability to see more deeply, I can then help students like Salvador compose their lives in schools as lives of fullness and hope. It is to that end that this book—and the practice it represents—is written. And to that end, I believe it will contribute to the practice of both teacher education and teaching in urban schools.

❖ NOTE

1. From *Woman Hollering Creek.* Copyright © 1991 by Sandra Cisneros. Published by Vintage Books, a division of Random House, Inc., New York, and originally in hardcover by Random House, Inc. Reprinted by permission of Susan Bergholz Literary Services, New York. All rights reserved.

❖ REFERENCES

Campano, G. (2003). *Reading Salvador and our reluctance to learn from others.* Unpublished manuscript, University of Indiana.

Cisneros, S. (1992). Salvador late or early. In *Woman Hollering Creek* (pp. 10–11). New York: Vintage.

1

Teaching and Learning to Teach as Principled Practice

Linda R. Kroll

Tomás Galguera

❖   ❖   ❖

My mind has struggled to name the terror in my repeated attempts to present well-considered lessons to a classroom of energetic yet challenging students. Half of my struggle is against myself and my own expectation that I can't handle such "difficult" kids. A portion of my struggle is comprised of sheer exhaustion and the emotional cost of repeatedly putting myself out there; scrambling to quickly learn to crawl, stumble, walk, and then run in the 40-yard dash that is the construction of a new teacher's knowledge of the world and work of an educator. Certainly I struggle with the enormity of a small classroom full of 35 fifteen-year-olds and the intricacies of how to both keep their attention and teach them something. Finally, there is the emotional toll of caring so much about what my students and I are experiencing, both apart and together.

> *My hope is to find the proper process with which to move all this information through my brain in a way that will facilitate developing the magic answer that will save me in the midst of the chaos. My fear is that I will end this year by abandoning these kids in favor of my emotional health and well-being. I have been close, in the past few weeks, to giving up and giving in. It is truly a struggle. And still, I feel incapable of naming or explaining most of it.*[1]
>
> —Debra Perrin, first-year high school English teacher

Few professions can promise as much reward, and guarantee as much challenge, as teaching. Few experiences are as satisfying as being responsible for a student's learning, for the satisfaction and pride that pours out of students' eyes at the magical "aha!" moment. Yet, few endeavors can be as complex and pose as much a threat to one's sense of self-efficacy, especially because to teach students what is essential for them to know in the best way possible, all of society must change first; and public education is the very institution through which change is to occur. How can we solve this conundrum?

Learning to teach is a lifelong commitment. Teaching teachers is an enormous responsibility. Mindful of the enormity of our task as teacher educators at Mills College, we move forward, observing, probing, caring, talking, thinking about what and how we teach and its implications. One could say that our charge extends beyond making sure that teachers such as Debra have the wherewithal to keep from "giving up and giving in" to the overwhelming challenge that teaching, especially in poor, urban schools, represents. Our responsibility ultimately rests with Debra's students and the thousands of students taught by the teachers we teach. We are responsible for making sure that all these students, as a result of the very thoughts, feelings, actions, and words of their teachers, live in a more equitable and just society. This is the fundamental principle that guides our practice.

In this book, we show, for example, not merely how learning to teach can be framed by the standards outlined by the State of California and administered by the State Commission for Teacher Credentialing, but also how it can be guided by a set of principles dedicated to social justice as reflected in excellent outcomes and equitable opportunities for youth and children in urban public schools. These principles are designed to work together in the interest of ambitious teaching practice that addresses squarely the needs of all learners. Our teacher education practice reflects our urban setting in Oakland, California. So do our coupled commitments to equity and social justice. We believe that in spite of the many extraordinary problems facing schools—and in the large urban environment where we are located, there are, indeed, many—these institutions hold more promise than others for redistributing wealth and opportunity in our country and for reinvigorating our democratic ideal.

The authors of this book have been working with a vision for effective urban education for many years, some of us since 1988. Others have come on board over the years. Each time a new person joins the faculty in the Department of Education at Mills College, the vision of social justice, equity, and excellent outcomes for all children has been refined and clarified. We began with three big ideas: inquiry and reflective practice as essential to good teaching, a knowledge of developmental theory as a way of understanding how people learn, and a determination that the teachers we prepared would be agents of change in the schools. As we worked together and gained new input, other big ideas developed until we reached (for the moment) our six principles:

- Teaching is a moral act founded on an ethic of care.
- Teaching is an act of inquiry and reflection.
- Learning is a constructivist/developmental process.
- The acquisition of subject matter and content knowledge is essential.
- Teaching is a collegial act and requires collaboration.
- Teaching is essentially a political act.

These six principles have provided a set of lenses that help us to understand our practice and goals as we strive to help teachers learn to create classrooms in which social justice, equity, and powerful learning can occur. The principles can provide us with a way to move forward, to generate reasonable, effective responses to the expected and unexpected challenges of teaching.

Few institutions in our society have as much power to influence beliefs, values, and behavior as schools. Consequently, the expectations for what schools can do for society are legion. Schools are expected to educate the population so that its members can realize the American dream of a democratic society, where all people have affluent and meaningful lives, characterized by human rights and freedoms unheard of in many parts of the world. Yet, schools are currently seen as failing the students they serve and not fulfilling the promise of producing a literate, reflective, well-educated population that can participate intelligently in a democratic society. The historical promise of American public schools is that they should be available to all and provide the opportunity and support for all children to realize their full potential. However, historically, this promise has been inequitably fulfilled, with countless students struggling to make sense of schools that are unable to support their development and the blossoming of their full capacities and, instead, often segregate and brand them according to criteria that reflect societal biases. This inequity leads to social injustice for many American children, their families, and the communities from which they come. As a result, schools, as they currently exist, do not fulfill their historical promise and mission (Darling-Hammond, 1997; Gardner, 1991; Haberman, 2000). We must re-envision the potential of public education and the mission of the public school.

The key to that outcome, we believe, is you, the teachers who teach or will teach in those schools. You must be well prepared, both in the subject matters you teach and in ways to transform that subject matter into meaningful learning opportunities for your students. You must be acutely aware of the moral nature of your work and your responsibility to act in the best interest of your students and the students' families, as well as their communities. Given the complexity of your work and its inherently political nature, you must be prepared to work productively in schools as they are and to participate in creating them anew. This requires that you are equipped to learn as well as to teach and that your professional reflective capabilities are keen. Knowing that you are not alone in the work of teaching is important as well. If you accept the enormity of the task as we have described it here, then you know that your capacity for building a community of practice is not marginal to the work—rather it is central.

In this book, we talk about preparing teachers with this set of knowledge and skills as well as with the disposition to do what must be done. In this time of increased regulation and standardization, we believe it is critical to put another voice forward—one that embraces the need for high standards and powerful school and university practice, one that believes the road to getting there is the careful conceptualization of what the work of teaching entails and the construction of an integrated set of learning experiences to get there.

A principled practice approach to teacher education differs from both what has happened historically and what is being asked of most teacher-education programs today. Historically, teacher-education programs were expected to verify that teachers had achieved a certain level of competency in specific areas (such as the teaching of reading or classroom management). How those levels were to be achieved and how that was to be judged were up to each program to demonstrate. This approach, while attempting to be all-encompassing, was fragmented, failing to provide teachers with an integrated sense they could use to judge their own practice once they were certified. A more recent move has been toward the identification and codification of standards for teacher-education programs and their graduates. This model, too, has for the most part resulted in a fragmented, disconnected view of what needs to be done. It is not that the common standards outlined by state departments of education are not important; it is that the way in which they are articulated again fails to help teachers see how the whole may fit together. Throughout the United States, state legislation has mandated new standards for "qualified" teachers that are applicable to both beginning and experienced teachers. These standards are simultaneously specific and inclusive of a broad range of connected ideas. They include, for example, general teaching standards (for example, the California standards for the teaching profession), frameworks and standards for each subject matter, teaching performance expectations for beginning teachers, and standardized assessments to judge teaching performance. However, all these standards and assessments are focused primarily on what is at the surface of teaching: classroom environment, lesson planning, individualization of instruction, assessment, and diagnosis. All of these surface features are extremely important, but when they are effective, they are the result of reflection and understanding of a set of moral and political ideas that are not articulated in the standards. Hence, the standards contain hidden assumptions and conclusions that can prevent teachers from continuing to develop and to learn.

In a way, we see similarities between how one learns to teach and how one learns a language. One way to think about learning a language is in terms of mastering its surface features: sounds, words, utterances, and phrases. After all, speaking a language is about being able to produce appropriate sounds, words, utterances, and phrases. It would seem to follow, then, that teaching a language should consist mostly of modeling and providing students with opportunities to practice producing it. This is a familiar process for millions of people visiting a foreign country, who struggle to learn a few essential expressions so they can carry on with their daily activities. *Wie geht's* or *Necesito ayuda, por favor* become essential first steps for second-language learners. However, true language learning only takes place when learners get beyond pragmatic needs and begin taking apart these prefabricated chunks of language. Languages are governed by principles that are more or less specific to certain languages or language groups, by grammars (not necessarily the rules one learns in school) that one must learn to go beyond a limited range of utterances and expressions. Similarly, beginning teachers learn "tricks" and useful systems of classroom management, teach prefabricated curriculum and published materials. However, it is not until they begin to understand the norms and basic assumptions that govern the behavior not only of teachers but also of students that they truly begin to learn to teach. A principled approach to teacher education is how we aim to familiarize students explicitly with the grammar of teaching and learning. Becoming proficient in a second language consists of more than simply developing a native-like accent. We now know that becoming proficient in a language is a cognitive process. In other words, more than sounding right, we need to understand how a language works. The particular six principles we rely on are not the grammar itself; rather, they serve as scaffolds for us to apprentice[2] beginning teachers into teaching, a most complex profession. We are not satisfied with preparing teachers who behave like teachers. We need to make sure that we prepare teachers who understand teaching deeply.

A principled approach to understanding teaching can help you to build a framework in which you can better understand and control your work. The principles get at what is at the essence of teaching: relationships, subject matter, learning and development, context for learning and teaching. All of these get represented and acted out in specific ways when we think about them in relation to any of the legislated standards, but the principles help you to think about your teaching in deeper and more powerful ways. They provide a touchstone for each of us—beginning teachers, experienced teachers, teacher educators—to evaluate and consider our practice within a widening set of arenas, including the classroom, the school, the community, and the larger political arena. In addition to providing us with the opportunity for focused reflection on practice, the principles enable us to generate solutions to identified issues. They allow us a responsive, flexible approach, as opposed to a formulized, recipe-like set of solutions. This may mean that we have to think longer and harder, even when we have no time to do so, and that we are likely to make lots of mistakes along the way. The advantage of using principles is the touchstone quality of having a gauge by which we can consider and reconsider our practice.

The principles have operated in that manner for us. As teacher educators, each time we teach a lesson we are able to ask ourselves: What are the moral consequences of what we are doing and asking the students to do? How does this particular activity or discussion or set of readings reflect the notion of an ethic of care? In thinking about our lessons in this way, we engage in reflective practice. However, we need to think purposefully about inquiry as part of our work on a regular basis. So as we teach, we ask ourselves: What essential question can we think about based on what we are teaching? What do we want to know about our students' learning and development from this activity? Our questions require us to look at how our students are learning and how they are interacting with the content we teach them. We ask ourselves: Which students are engaged in what ways with this content? What does this tell us about the nature of what we are trying to teach? What are the larger consequences of learning or not learning this material? Which power structures does our teaching represent and support and which does it exclude and undermine? The principles provide us, as educators, with a set of lenses with which to view our own practice and with which to think about the practice of our preservice teachers.

These principles not only act as lenses through which we can consider our teaching and our students' learning but also help us to generate what it is we want to teach. Thus, for example, if we are teaching preservice teachers to teach reading, we can ask ourselves: What are the moral components of this task? What do we know about the ways people learn, and particularly the ways they learn to read, that can help us think about how and what to teach? The answers we find to these questions help us to think about what to teach in the area of learning to teach reading. Although our six principles constitute a philosophical stance that we take toward education in general and teacher education specifically, they are not without an empirical foundation. As we explain in subsequent chapters, each principle embodies a facet of what we have learned about teaching and about preparing teachers in light of our commitment to equity and social justice. Each principle is also informed by relevant research and theories. We strive to prepare the best teachers possible for urban schools, guided not by blind ideology but by informed conviction. At the same time, our concern toward clearly articulating our objectives as well as the conceptual framework behind each objective compels us to recognize that, however powerful it is, there are costs and limitations in adopting a principled approach to educating teachers.

One potential pitfall of a principled approach to teacher education is that these principles may become rhetoric, a sort of jargon that marks users as in-group members. We are all too familiar with similar situations, in which particular words and terms are the result of the latest fad sweeping American education. Teachers often judge colleagues solely on the basis of whether they are fluent in the latest acronyms and terminology. Not only is this possibility counter to our collegiality principle but also it leads to a superficial understanding of crucial issues in education. To prevent our principles from becoming cursory jargon, we refer to them in various contexts and teach them from diverse perspectives. The chapters that follow demonstrate the different ways you might think about each of these principles in a variety of circumstances. While we can develop and encourage the development of basic questions that are inspired by the principles, we emphasize the context-specific nature of the answers to these questions. Our approach has similarities with authentic and communicative approaches to teaching vocabulary. Thus, we do not simply teach our preservice teachers a list of principles for them to memorize and regurgitate in examinations. Rather, we refer to these principles time and again in reflecting on their experiences and practice, until they begin to use the principles to talk about their own experiences. As you read this book, ask yourself questions that will enable you to understand the principles beyond the words we use.

The peril also exists that beginning teachers may interpret our principles as dogma to be followed without question. We are aware that, because we make them a central feature of our own teacher-education program, our beginning teachers may think of our six principles as "self-evident truths." Such a position is enticing because believing something to be true excuses us from examining it critically. Furthermore, dogmatic positions foster feelings of privilege and elitism that also run counter to our overarching principle of equity and social justice. We don't want our principles to be misconstrued as dogma. As we go along, we will ask you to question what you are reading, so that even in this limited context you can engage in reflection and critical analysis of your own learning and teaching in light of the six principles. Again, we will try to provide you with opportunities as you read the text parallel to the questions we ask of our preservice teachers. We are also quite explicit in telling our own preservice teachers that we have revised our principles and are likely to do so in the future, precisely because they are neither fully adequate yet, nor are they likely ever to be.

Relying on a fixed set of principles to understand and talk about learning and teaching in the context of public schools also has the potential of limiting our ability to fully appreciate the complexity of the phenomenon we examine. All knowledge has the characteristic of being reductionist in that it defines our perception. For instance, our belief that learning is a constructivist process in fact prevents us from seeing learning as anything but a constructivist process. We are aware of this. However, we also realize that we gain much from thinking about learning in this manner. Seeing learning as being socially co-constructed provides us with a powerful model not only for understanding ways in which our students and all students learn but also for guiding our teaching and that of our students. At least until we find more powerful theories or ways to think about learning and teaching, we will rely on our principles as six possible lenses and descriptors for looking at and talking about our own and our preservice teachers' work.

Finally, we realize that we cannot go on adding principles to our list, regardless of how many distinct facets we are able to identify in our quest to prepare the best possible teachers for urban schools. At present, our six principles seem sufficient. Still, the process since its beginning has been additive, and it remains to be seen how many principles may be too many. Similarly, as we further understand our task as teacher educators, we may choose to split one of the principles into two or more subcomponents. One way to prevent our principles from becoming an unwieldy or cumbersome list is for us to constantly assess their usefulness. Similarly, we need to be somewhat conservative in deciding to add principles to our list. This should not be taken to mean that we have been impulsive when adding new principles. New principles have been added only when we were able to define them and articulate a strong argument for their usefulness and appropriateness.

Despite the possible limitations and potential problems of a principled approach to preparing teachers, we have ample evidence suggesting that the advantages of this approach clearly outweigh the costs. Use of the principles provides a guided opportunity for reflection on and in practice, allowing for the generation of new practice, and giving a common understanding that must be made explicit in each context. In subsequent chapters, we present selected illustrations of the power of a principled approach to teacher education. However, before you begin reading about each of the principles individually, we will describe them as a whole, briefly, and consider what questions they might raise for you as you read through the following chapters.

❖ THE PRINCIPLES

We present the following brief summaries and questions to help us paint the landscape we will explore in greater detail in subsequent chapters. Although this territory is by no means exhaustive or even fully mapped, the principles represent our effort both to prepare the best teachers possible for tomorrow's schools and to understand and imagine our practice as teacher educators. The nature of this effort has led us to a set of interrelated principles. Thus, some of the ideas or questions may seem to be overlapping. This overlap indicates the organic and linked nature of this set of ideas.

Teaching Is a Moral Act Founded on an Ethic of Care

What does it mean to say that teaching is a moral act? At the root of this principle is the idea that all teaching is based on trusting relationships. Teachers have relationships with their students, their students' families and communities, and their colleagues. In relationships based on trust, we try to act in the best interest of everyone concerned. This is not always so easy to do, and the best interest of everyone may not always be evident. Thus, this principle reminds us to ask questions with regard to our actions and decisions such as:

- What are the consequences of this action? Who will benefit? Who will suffer? In what ways?
- What are the goals I have for taking this action? How will this best serve my students? What will their families think? What about my colleagues?
- What will my students learn from this action? Will this action deepen the trust in our relationship? How will they understand what I am doing?

In reading the chapter on teaching as a moral act, try to consider some of these questions as you read along, thinking about your own teaching and learning experiences. Try to vary your focus from you as the teacher to your potential or current students and their families and to your potential or current colleagues.

Teaching Is an Act of Inquiry and Reflection

This principle reminds us to regard our teaching simultaneously as research and instruction. It reminds us to pause in the process of making decisions and finding problem solutions. Typically, when confronted with a dilemma or problem, we like to solve it and move on to the next thing. Unfortunately, jumping directly to a solution may keep us from really addressing what is happening. If we inquire into our practice, try to understand what is really happening, and reflect on what we conclude, our solutions to problems may be very different from the ones we jump to without such considerations. This principle encourages us to make inquiry a habit of mind. To do so, we might think about questions such as:

- What is really happening here? How do I know? What evidence do I have?
- What else could it be? What other evidence is there that might support this alternative interpretation?
- What other evidence can I gather to check out these different possibilities?

Questions such as these help us to keep focused on inquiry and reflection as we teach and as we learn. As you read the chapter on teaching as an act of inquiry, try to think of examples of problems either in your own classroom or in the classroom where you are the student where these questions could help you better understand what is happening.

Learning Is a Constructivist/Developmental Process

Historically, there have been three different perspectives on the nature of learning: a behavioral/environmental explanation, a nativist/ evolutionary explanation, and an interactionist/constructivist/developmental explanation. None of these perspectives is any longer uniquely followed. It is recognized that all of them contain some of the truth. However, American education has long been modeled on a behaviorist explanation of how children learn. This explanation can lead to the belief that when you tell someone something, they hear what you have said and learn it as you presented it. We don't believe that learning works that way. On the contrary, we believe that each of us brings to a learning situation a host of previous experiences that will influence how we interpret that situation and what we will make of it. Thus, each of us *constructs* for ourselves our own understanding, influenced by, among other things, our own previous experience, our own language, our own culture, and our own community or social experiences.

The principle or belief that learning is a constructivist/developmental process encourages us to ask the following kinds of questions as we teach:

- What do I hope my students will understand from this lesson? How do I know that they are ready to understand the lesson in this way? What evidence do I have?
- When I ask my students questions, are their answers related to what I have asked? What question are they answering? If they are answering a different question, what does this tell me about what they do and do not understand?
- If they give the "correct" answer, how can I be clear on what it is they understand about the issue at hand? What evidence do I need?
- What do I know about these particular students and the ways that they learn? What does developmental theory tell me about children this age? What particular things do I know about them, their families, their communities, their language, their interests and passions that will help me figure out how to engage them in what I am required to teach them?
- In what ways has my understanding of the content, students, and my practice changed as a result of my teaching?

Questions such as these help us to focus on the learner as we teach. They help us to think about what is going on for our students even as we concentrate on what we teach. As you read this chapter, think about when these questions might be most useful to you.

The Acquisition of Subject Matter and Content Knowledge Is Essential

In some ways, this principle may seem the most obvious. If you are going to teach, you must teach something. If we are committed to an agenda of social justice and equitable opportunities and excellent outcomes for all students, then we must take seriously what we teach and how we teach it. We need to think about the nature of the discipline we are teaching and what its fundamental questions are. We need to think about whom we are teaching and the match between the nature of the discipline and our particular students. We need to think about what the state or district expects of us in terms of curriculum and pedagogy and coordinate that with what we believe to be the best for our students with regard to content and instruction. Questions such as the following can be posed:

- In what ways has my understanding of the content, students, and my practice changed as a result of my teaching?
- What do I understand about the nature of the discipline? What does it mean to know mathematics or literature? What does it mean to be a scientist or a historian? How can I give my students the opportunity to try this on?
- How does my curriculum reflect my learners' experiences and understanding?

As you read the chapter on subject matter, raise questions like these for yourself about your own teaching and learning experiences and about your own efforts to create and adapt appropriate and effective curriculum and pedagogy.

Teaching Is a Collegial Act and Requires Collaboration

We have said quite a bit already about the importance of relationships in teaching and the importance of inquiry and reflection. Knowledge, we believe, is socially constructed; much of what we learn we learn with others, even if the ultimate construction is an individual endeavor. Thus, our colleagues and our students and their families are instrumental in our learning, as well in their own. This principle focuses on how teaching is collegial and what collaboration can do to help us teach better and to continue to learn more about our own practice. As you read about this principle and reflect on your own practice, you might keep some of the following questions in mind:

- What have others done to teach this subject matter to students like mine? Who at my school site might want to collaborate with me on this curriculum?
- Has anyone else struggled with a child with these particular needs or interests? Who can I confer with to help me teach this child the best way I can?
- What opportunities can I find for bringing up important issues (issues of equity, for example) in a way that will have all of us

working together on the issue in a productive way? What can I learn from others about this issue?

- At our grade level (or department) meetings, what can I do to ensure that we work productively on big-idea questions?
- What are my responsibilities to students, their families, my colleagues, administrators, and other members of my professional community? How can they help me in my teaching?

Thinking about opportunities for collaboration and collegiality can lead to powerful knowing on the part not only of teachers but also of children, as teachers pool their understandings and challenge each other's assumptions. The support and enjoyment that can be gained from collegial relationships are among the most satisfying aspects of teaching. Collegiality and collaboration can help create schools that are places of lifelong learning for the adults who work in them as well as for the children and families who are their clientele.

Teaching Is Essentially a Political Act

Early in this introduction, we put forward the notion that major societal and political changes can be effected by schools and schooling. This principle makes that notion explicit and helps us to think about how the political nature of teaching is manifested moment to moment on a daily basis. In the chapter that focuses on this principle, we use a particular example to illustrate what we mean by this, but it is important to remember that each act you make as a teacher has a political meaning and consequence. Thus, as you think about this principle and your teaching, you might ask yourself the following questions:

- In choosing to teach this curriculum from this perspective, whose points of view am I highlighting and whose am I neglecting? How can I make sure to include other perspectives?
- Are the curricula and pedagogies I use accessible and meaningful in various ways to all my students?
- What do I know about the political and cultural experiences of the community of this school? What experiences are common for the children and their families? How are they like or unlike experiences with which I myself am familiar?
- How are families enfranchised or disenfranchised by the school district and school regulations? How do parents or other family members interact with the school and its personnel? How can I

contribute to a positive experience for the children I teach and their families?

- What are institutional or cultural beliefs about the subject matter I am teaching? How do these coordinate with what I believe about how students will best learn this content?
- Is my authority as a teacher enhancing my students' capacity to become active and contributing members of society? Besides my role in the classroom, what else do I do that has political consequences for me and my students?

Cobb, Wood, and Yackel (1993) point out that to fully understand what happens in a classroom, one must consider not only the relationship between individual knowledge and institutionalized practices but also the broader sociopolitical setting and the function of the school as a societal institution. Cobb et al. are speaking of the teaching of mathematics, but their statement could apply to any discipline. As you read the chapter on teaching as political, raise questions for yourself about what is political about what you are teaching and how that political nature is manifested in your everyday classroom life.

Each of these chapters provides you with a different lens to think about the nature of teaching and learning, both for your students and for yourselves as teachers. The chapters serve to make explicit the richness and complexity of the act of teaching. The principles provide us with an integrated, explicit, and deep way to think about the work we do, as well as its significance not only for ourselves and our individual students but also for the communities we serve. We continue to believe that these principles will help us change schools to serve the democratic ideals that they profess. We also hope that you will join us in a larger conversation about what it means to learn to teach and prepare future teachers who will fulfill the lofty yet worthy promise of education to create a better world for all. Neither we nor any one group of educators has the answer to the complex and vexing challenges facing schools these days. Thus, we invite you to critically consider the positions and perspectives that this book represents and engage in appropriate, thoughtful action.

❖ NOTES

1. Reprinted with permission from Debra Perrin.
2. We use *apprentice* in agreement with cognitive apprenticeship models, in which apprentices are taught "to think like experts" (Collins, Brown, & Newman, 1989, p. 488).

❖ REFERENCES

Cobb, P., Wood, T., & Yackel, E. (1993). Discourse, mathematical thinking, and classroom practice. In E. Forman, N. Minick, & C. A. Stone (Eds.), *Contexts for learning: Sociocultural dynamics in children's development* (pp. 91–119). New York: Oxford University Press.

Collins, A., Brown, J. S., & Newman, S. E. (1989). Cognitive apprenticeship: Teaching the crafts of reading, writing, and mathematics. In L. B. Resnick (Ed.), *Knowing, learning, and instruction: Essays in honor of Robert Glaser* (pp. 453–494). Hillsdale, NJ: Lawrence Erlbaum.

Darling-Hammond, L. (1997). *The right to learn: A blueprint for creating schools that work.* San Francisco: Jossey-Bass.

Gardner, H. (1991). *The unschooled mind: How children think and how schools should teach them.* New York: Basic Books.

Haberman, M. (2000). Urban schools: Day camps or custodial centers? *Phi Delta Kappan, 82*(3), 203–208.

2

Learning to Negotiate the Moral Terrain of Teaching

Anna Ershler Richert

❖ ❖ ❖

S everal days ago, Marie, a novice teacher colleague of mine, came
to talk with me about a group of four students in her high school
history class who plagiarized their end-of-the-term book reports. She
wanted to "think out loud" about what she should do. She explained
that the problem began when Avi, a young Pakistani student who was
the author of the original paper, "loaned" her book report to a group of
three girls in her class with whom she was trying to establish friend-
ships. By the time the four final book reports reached Marie, all read
very much the same, which caused her to agonize over what she
should do. The details of the circumstances that faced Marie help
explain the agony she felt.

Each girl's situation presented a unique challenge. Sonia, for example, one of the three who copied the report, is a recent immigrant from

---

AUTHOR'S NOTE: All the names used in this chapter are pseudonyms.

Nicaragua who does not speak much English. She explained to Marie that reading and rewording the report was what she thought the assignment actually entailed. She was surprised by Marie's concern. Paula, the second of the three—who Marie noted is absent from class more than she is there—expressed pride in completing this work; it was the first assignment she had turned in since the school year began. While Nikki, the third girl of the three recognized her infraction, she was unclear about "why it was such a big deal." She had not copied the report "directly," she claimed, but rather she used it as a "resource" in constructing her own report. She said she didn't care about what would happen because she expected to fail the course anyway.

The dilemma concerning Avi herself was no less troubling. In fact, what action to take regarding her became more complex when Marie realized that the school's procedure for plagiarism was to contact the students' parents. Currently, Avi lives in the United States, not with her parents but with relatives who Avi claims are not interested in her progress at school. Her mother died several years earlier in a car crash in which Avi herself was severely scarred on half her body and face. Her father, who lives in Pakistan, eagerly awaits his daughter's return. He has promised her hand in marriage, a gesture that will secure her a husband, which is something he is concerned about, given the disfigurement the accident caused. Every day his daughter remains in the United States completing her education is too long as far as he is concerned. For Avi, it's too short. Both Avi's suitor and her dowry await her arrival in Pakistan. Whereas her father wants her home, Avi dreads going back.

❖ MANAGING MORAL DILEMMAS

Every day, teachers face complex moral dilemmas like the one Marie faces in this case. The dilemmas are moral in nature because they occur inside a triangle of relationships between the teacher, the student, and the subject matter, for which the teacher holds primary responsibility (Ball & Cohen, 1999; Hawkins, 1974; McDonald, 1992). Within this triangle of constant interactions, teachers are expected to manage matters and ultimately act in the "best interest" of their students. The problem is that what is in the best interest of any particular student at any particular time is neither easily defined nor readily determined.

The difficulty teachers face lies in dealing with the complexity of these dilemmas. Typically, problems involve an array of circumstances that are not fully known to the teacher. How the families of the four girls in Marie's class will react to hearing of their daughters' problems at school provides an example. Will they support their child in learning when it is proper to copy and when it is not (assuming that they even know these conventions in the first place), or how to cite sources properly, or in gaining the skills necessary to do their writing and original work? Or will they punish the girls for not doing what they "ought to do" as defined by their teacher and school?

Even when the teacher does understand many of the circumstances surrounding any particular case, the multiple layers of complexity are still difficult to disentangle for each child. When more than one student is involved, the complexity is heightened. Any action Marie decides to take in this case will have different consequences for each of those involved. When several students are implicated—as is typically the case in the complex setting of school and as is the case here—a chain of consequences is likely to follow. In these circumstances, the set of consequences unfolds like a house of tumbling cards, with each careening into the next. The overall impact is difficult to predict.

Anticipating these consequences is part of the moral work of teaching—and a part that makes it so extraordinarily hard to do. There is almost never a clear-cut, right-or-wrong answer to be had when resolving moral dilemmas—or an easily definable right-or-wrong action to take. Some have argued that because of these layers of uncertainty, dilemmas such as the one faced by Marie are not problems that can be "solved" but rather "dilemmas that must be managed" (Cuban, 2001; Lampert, 1985). Managing them is clearly one of the most difficult aspects of teachers' work.

The Inherently Moral Nature of Teaching as Work

The moral nature of teaching connects in direct and important ways with the goal of teaching: creating opportunities for students to learn. Teachers are morally obligated to create a classroom and curriculum that will open the doors of learning to their students. But what students are to learn, or when, or at what cost, or for whose benefit, are never easy to determine. This difficulty is due to the different and changing needs of students, as well as the relational context within which teachers come to know them and their learning needs. Each child a teacher encounters is different from all the others encountered every day. Because each child is his or her own unique self, teachers have to learn to account for the individual differences among children all day long.

Still, it would be simpler if those differences among people were the only factor contributing to the moral complexity of teaching as work. They are not. The changing world of which schools are a part adds to the complexity of the work of teaching as well. Students change from moment to moment and day to day. The relationships between teachers and their students shift and change, as do the relationships between teachers, students, and the subject matter they teach. Not only the students themselves but also how those students view the subjects they study may change.

Similarly, teachers also change: They know their subject matters more and less well, their students more and less well, and their contexts more or less well. Even the subject matter changes in important and sometimes unpredictable ways. New concepts are discovered in every discipline, and ways of conceiving of the discipline change over time. These changes all combine to make this triangle of teaching relationships messy, according to McDonald (1992), who characterizes teaching as managing "the teacher's own ambivalent self, that bunch of unpredictable kids, and the always slippery subject matter" (p. 13). How to act in the best interest of children is difficult, indeed, given the shifting, uncertain, and complex context within which teaching occurs.

❖ MARIE'S DILEMMA

Avi's situation illustrates both the moral nature of the dilemmas embedded in teachers' work and the layers of complexity brought about by the relationships involved in doing this work well. Analyzing it will set the stage for us to think about how to deliberate over matters of moral concern and how to support one another to act in morally responsible ways. We will begin by looking closely at the dilemma Marie faced in deciding what to do in this instance and how to think through the set of relationships she had with this cluster of four girls in her history class. What we can see immediately is how the moral dimensions of teaching—the principle we are considering in this chapter—overlap and intersect with the other principles of teaching we discuss in this book. The fact that resolving this case required much deliberate and careful thinking on Marie's part illustrates the reflective nature of teaching, for example. The fact that she came to me to discuss her thoughts illustrates the collaborative nature of the work. That Marie's central concern is about how students who copy one another's papers are less likely to be constructing new ideas of their own under-scores how a constructivist learning theory guides her practice. None of the principles described in this volume stands alone: In considering instances of practice, it becomes clear how they come together to help us understand our complex work and take action that is aligned with what we believe.

Considering the Relationships Involved in Avi's Case

Over several months, Marie created a learning context in her class-room that had students studying the history texts of the class in various ways: alone, with her, and with one another. Within the context of these subject matter-bound relationships, Marie believed her students would be able to accomplish the learning goals she set for them. Her own relationship with the students was an important part of the array. She believed that to teach them to learn history, for example, or to appreci-ate the value of creating their own original work—about plagiarism and what it means—she needed to know them well. She needed to have a sense of what they understood of the course materials and what they did not understand, what aspects of the work they found difficult and what parts came more easily to them, what other factors in their lives impacted their ability to engage or not, and so forth.

Whereas the student/teacher relationship was centrally important to the learning opportunities in Marie's class, it was not the only rela-tionship of importance. Also important were the relationships between the students. What Marie knew of the friendship relationships added another layer of complexity to her decision about how to act. For one thing, she knew how important these relationships were to Avi, who had struggled all year to establish friendships with the girls and to find a place for herself in the school. In some ways, Marie saw the friend-ships as supporting the girls' learning by providing a way for them to accomplish work they would not otherwise do. At the same time, these same relationships subverted their learning. Three of the four girls did not appear to do much original thinking about the book they suppos-edly read; much of the essay construction and actual writing seemed to fall on the shoulders of one. In the end, Marie worried that the students who copied the paper were not learning to use historical methods to think and to write. Nor had they learned the academic principle of authoring one's own work. Whereas all three of Avi's friends sidestepped the requirement that they do the reading and thinking on their own, the fact that they turned to one another in friendship was not irrelevant.

The friendship relationships that were developed in Marie's history class were important to her as they supported collaboration, which was one of her goals for her students. She recalled delivering her "we-are-not-in-this-alone" speech often in class to encourage students to help one another grapple with the complex questions they confronted in their texts. In addition to learning history, learning to learn together was an explicit goal of the course. As she sorted through the issues surrounding the plagiarism case she could not help but wonder if she might have been responsible—or partially so—for the students not understanding fully that collaboration was not called for (nor acceptable) for the learning task here.

Considering the Context

The context of Marie's work was significant, too, in her deliberation over the case. By *context*, we mean the context of the school, which has rules and regulations, many explicit and others not, which govern how things happen or "ought to happen" as teachers do their work. Similarly, the context of the profession of teaching also has rules and regulations about how teachers need to act and what kinds of responsibilities they have for ensuring the education, well-being, and safety of the children they serve. In reasoning through moral dilemmas, teachers must consider the larger context as well as the details of any particular case. Neither schools nor the profession of teaching is neutral, even though textbooks about teaching and many state and national documents describe the work as if it were. Rather, there are power differentials in school settings that add to the moral complexity of the work that goes on there. This is why context matters as we consider the moral nature of our work.

In considering Marie's dilemma, for example, the truth is that she has power over her students. She will determine the consequences of their having plagiarized their work. She (with the help of her school policies, of course) will determine what will happen to Avi and her friends as a result of their actions. Their lives will be directly impacted by what she decides is "right" to do. At the moment of decision regarding these girls, the power lies in Marie's hands. Not only does she have the power to act, as their teacher, she is obligated to do so.

Power, Action, and Consequences

Knowing she has this power is not easy for Marie. She agonizes over what action to take. She reasons that she could call her students' homes; or give them failing grades; or provide them "another chance." Each option suggests an opportunity to learn—but for each, there are negative consequences as well. Seldom are the consequences of a teacher's actions without meaning in the child's life. If Marie calls Avi's family, there is a distinct possibility that the child will be sent back to Pakistan. If she fails the previously failing students, chances are she will confirm their already low self-esteem. If she was not clear about when collaboration is appropriate and when it is not, she will be punishing students for something she had a hand in making occur. In every instance, the students' lives will be impacted by the decision she makes. She is morally obligated to use that power well.

Although answers to questions about what actions to take to ensure learning outcomes for children are seldom clear, teachers are still required to make determinations and to act. We know that prescriptions about what to do typically don't account for context and are therefore ineffectual. We also know that children and subject matter always change, making the need for teachers to change critical, as well. In this context of uncertainty, teachers are called on to employ professional judgment as they establish learning relationships that will create learning opportunities for their students. Finding out how to create a caring classroom where all children will have opportunities to learn is a critically important aspect of learning to teach. We turn next to developing the knowledge, skills, and dispositions needed to create such a classroom and to negotiate teaching's moral terrain.

❖ DEVELOPING THE SKILLS OF MORAL PRACTICE IN TEACHING

Learning to grapple with the moral underpinnings of teaching is part of the lifelong process of learning to teach. Both novice and veteran teachers must continuously ask themselves why they take the actions they do and what the consequences of those actions are for their students and others whom their decision impacts. This constant examination of purposes and consequences is a habit of mind that teachers must develop early in their careers and practice throughout. Establishing and developing this questioning or reflective stance is central to professional growth. With this stance, teachers begin to grapple with the moral questions that are ubiquitous in their work.

As we consider teaching closely, it becomes clearer just how full of moral deliberation it is. What might be less clear at this point is how to learn to approach the work of teaching in this way and to reason through these moral dilemmas to a place of responsible action. Thinking through Avi's case causes us to ask ourselves what it takes to do this aspect of the work of teaching well. What do the teachers need to know and be able to do? Whereas the answers to these questions could more than fill up a book of the size you are reading here, we might begin by identifying a set of habits of mind and action that will compel us down this path of morally responsible practice.

Recognizing the Moral Content of the Work

An important starting place in learning to approach teaching as moral work is to learn to recognize the moral content embedded in everyday practice. Everything a teacher does has consequences that are important to the people directly and indirectly connected to the case. The obvious recipients of the consequences are the involved students, of course. However, this is just where the consequences begin. Also impacted are the other students in the classroom (and sometimes the school, depending on the nature of the case), the parents of the children in the class, sometimes the other teachers in the school, and always the teacher herself. The moral content of teaching is ubiquitous. It is everywhere: in every action, every decision about what to teach and how, every encounter with a child, every interaction with a colleague.

Imagine the first two minutes of a first-period ninth-grade social studies class, for example. A student arrives late—not an uncommon occurrence in most classrooms. Every time any student arrives late, the teacher in charge has to decide how to deal with him or her. Let's think about what this teacher might do and what kind of thinking is required for taking that action. If the school has a tardy policy that says students cannot be late or they will be sent to the office, the teacher has to decide whether to uphold the rule (thus taking instructional minutes from those who arrived on time to attend to this child who did not) and send this particular tardy fellow to the office (where he or she, too, will miss out on valuable class time). Or, the teacher might decide to begin the class and talk with him later about needing to be punctual when it comes to attending class.

What else might be on her mind? She will probably consider whether or not the tardy behavior is typical for the student who is late. If this is the student's first time, then perhaps the teacher will let this instance slide. On the other hand, if tardiness is a schoolwide issue and the faculty has decided as a collective to grapple with it as a team, perhaps letting the infraction slide is not the decision to make. In that case, letting the infraction slide would be working against the spirit of building community across classrooms and grades. At the same time, if the student is new to the school and less familiar with the school policies— or new to the country, too—then she might choose to let the tardiness slide in spite of the schoolwide plan. Perhaps a private conference about what is required for success in school in this country would supercede the other possible actions that the teacher could take.

Obviously, it is not possible to go through all of the different ways the teacher might reason through this case. What is significant for our discussion here is that dilemmas such as these confront teachers all day long, from one moment to the next. And they matter, both to the student involved and to all the others in the classroom whose experience will be impacted as the teacher decides what to do. We can see from this example how moral deliberation is deeply embedded in the work of teaching. In this particular example, the teacher had many important decisions to make, and the school day was only two minutes old.

Recognizing the moral content of teaching is the first (and essential) step in learning to teach in a caring and responsible manner. However, the current push toward standardization and externally determined school agendas makes it difficult to attend to one's work in this way. As teachers are removed from making their own decisions about what to do, when, and for what purpose, they are removed from the core process of what teaching is all about. The approach we are advocating here places teachers back in the center of their work. Their careful reflective stance, leading to intentional action, is a core feature of teaching practice. In order for teachers to act as moral practitioners, they need to recognize the moral content of what they do and identify the moral dilemmas they need to resolve so that they can create caring relationships within which all students receive the education they deserve.

Resolving Dilemmas Rather Than Solving Problems

As we can see in our example, the dilemmas teachers face do not lend themselves to facile solutions. Even in a relatively simple situation such as the one we describe here, the complexities emerge quickly as one contemplates what action to take. The student in this instance was late to class—albeit only by a minute, let's say. This is a problem of sorts, yes, but not one that the teacher can solve. The fact is that the student was late. Although there is no problem for the teacher to solve, there is a dilemma to reason through: What should the teacher do about the student being late? Reflecting on a number of questions might be useful: How can I help the student not to be late again? How can I help the student realize why being on time is important? How can I use this as an opportunity to teach all of the students in the class about the school's new commitment to high expectations about punctuality and class time?

These are the kinds of questions that the teacher must begin to deliberate before deciding how to proceed. The particularities of any given case are also important. That the student we are considering here was only *one minute* late is relevant. After all, there is a good chance that the student's watch or the school clock is off by at least that much time. Also relevant is whether the student understood the school's procedures fully as a recently arrived immigrant student. Maybe the significance of the tardy policy and its importance in school attendance are not clear. The matter of the faculty's newly developed plan to set new standards and high expectations for student behavior is relevant to the case as well. It would be hard to step out of line if the faculty is working to have a consistent action for everyone in the school. Rather than solve this problem of one student being late, the teacher has to manage the dilemma it presents given the multiple circumstances that surround the case.

Part of learning to act in morally responsible ways involves understanding that the questions of practice typically present themselves as dilemmas with no direct, clear, or "right" answer. Furthermore, these dilemmas are value laden and require the weighing of consequences guided by moral principles and beliefs. Currently, the fast-paced, accountability-driven context of schools suggests that the problems of teaching are matters that can be quickly and efficiently solved, which makes moral deliberation difficult. As we saw in Marie's dilemma with Avi, and again in the example we've been considering here, many difficulties that teachers face do not lend themselves to quick and efficient solutions. In fact, many don't lend themselves to problem solving at all. Rather, these situations present themselves as deeply perplexing dilemmas with multiple and competing possibilities for action.

Reasoning Through Moral Dilemmas

This leads us to the next step in the process: learning to deliberate or reason through these perplexing circumstances. There are many ways to think about reasoning through moral dilemmas, but all of them involve teachers considering their *purposes*—both their larger purposes for teaching in the first place and their purposes with regard to any action at any particular point—and the *consequences* they anticipate for the actions they take. In our earlier example, we saw Marie reasoning through her choice of actions regarding Avi and her friends. We had a window onto some of her articulated purposes, which included learning to learn together as a stance toward learning history in her classroom, for example. We also had a window onto how she was thinking about the consequences she anticipated for the various actions she might take.

Anticipating the consequences of one's actions in teaching is an elaborate process. In part, this is because every classroom situation holds consequences for many people—some who are there when the action occurs, and others who are not but who will be impacted as well. In deciding what action to take with the late-arriving student described above, the teacher had to think about both the consequences for the student and those for the others in class who would witness her action and experience the possible time delays implicated in whatever she did. There would be consequences for the teacher, too. A new teacher, for example, might be thinking about how students will view him or her as a result of the action taken. Will they see their teacher as "tough" or "lenient," one who is "serious about the work of school" or one who "lets things slide"? And how about the consequences of the teacher's actions for the other teachers in the school, who have decided to have a united front when it comes to taking action on tardiness at their school? Part of the process of learning to teach in a morally responsible way is learning to anticipate the consequences for the people involved and then weigh those consequences against one's purposes. We could wish that, in the end of all careful deliberation, the choice about how to act would be easy; sadly, it almost never is.

Choosing How to Act

Choosing among the possible courses of action is the next step in the process. How do teachers choose how to act when there are so many competing circumstances and possibilities for what they might do? At this point in the process, teachers turn to some set of core ideas and beliefs, as well as a body of professional knowledge, to help guide them in their work. One's professional knowledge provides a foundation on which the choice of how to act might rest.

Relevant to every action choice is what teachers know about learning and subject matter and about the particular students involved in the case. What they know about how children learn and how one action or another will help their students acquire the knowledge, skills, and dispositions they are there to teach can guide them as they consider their action choices. In deliberating over the case of Avi, Marie drew on her knowledge of her students as adolescent learners of history. Whereas there are general things about learning history that were relevant to her in her deliberation—for example, that approaching questions of historical importance from multiple points of view is important—there were also particular issues and concerns about learning history in that class for those students, concerns that were important for her to consider as well. For example, that Avi is Pakistani rather than American was important when considering how she learns history and how she functions as a member of the community of learners in Marie's class. That Sonia is a recent immigrant whose English is limited was relevant as well, as Marie considered how she might approach the learning of history, what history she should learn, how the classroom work might be organized to help her access the class material, and so forth. Marie's professional knowledge was an important touchstone as she reasoned though this moral dilemma with Avi and her friends.

Two other places teachers might turn for guidance is to other teachers and to the school processes and procedures that typically outline how teachers "should" act in their work in schools. Veteran teachers have had to reason through countless moral dilemmas. In the process, many have become expert at anticipating consequences from different actions they might take. Turning to a trusted colleague whose work and judgment one admires is a helpful way to learn to reason through dilemmas and take action aligned with one's goals.

In a similar way, it is possible to get considerable guidance from school policies (formal and informal) and the school's general cultural norms, which typically highlight for teachers the school's stance about professional behavior and decision making. As we can see in Marie's case with Avi, where the school procedure required that parents be notified as a first step when plagiarism occurs, sometimes school procedures render the case more complex rather than clearer. Nevertheless, studying these policies is a good starting point when it comes to deciding how to act. They make available to teachers the legal steps that they must take in any particular case. In addition, they typically reflect the wisdom of practice of those who put them together for the school in the first place.

Turning to one's colleagues, or the official school procedures, or even one's developing body of professional knowledge, are all important steps in deciding how to act when one confronts the complexities of teaching. But ultimately, even with all that help, teachers have to make decisions about what to do in any given case based on what they value and believe. At this point, the moral nature of teaching comes into obvious view. Given that the choices for how to act are never clear, nor the consequences clear in advance of any action one takes, in the final moment, teachers need to turn inside themselves to decide what they believe would be professionally "right" to do. This involves drawing on a core set of values and commitments that teachers bring to teaching in the first place. Their sense of justice, their belief in an ethic of care, their commitment to honesty, and so forth are all values that they must ultimately draw on as they decide how they will act. The process is not only an intellectual one, but an emotional one as well. When all the reasoning and deliberation are done, and the weighing of values complete, only then can teachers decide what they will do. Deciding a course of action is an important step; taking action is something more.

The Courage to Act

Acting in accordance with one's beliefs in any professional setting is challenging, and it often takes all the courage one can muster. Why? For one, in teaching, professional actions are typically public actions about which everyone has an opinion. Only the person acting—in this case, the teacher—has full knowledge of why he or she chose to act in a particular way. People outside the action, who are watching what is done, will know only the part of the situation that is visible to them.

Given what they can see, they may not agree with what the teacher has decided to do. The culture of schooling is that those with different opinions typically let those opinions be known, which is hard on a teacher, especially a novice. It is not uncommon for a teacher to be confronted with much discussion about his or her action. It is almost impossible to avoid having some constituent unhappy with the choice.

Since choice always involves tradeoffs, furthermore, it is also difficult for the teacher to feel clear and confident when choosing an action to take. In the case of Avi, Marie decided in the end to meet with the four girls and talk with them about plagiarism and why it is wrong. She did not call their parents, nor did she give them failing grades. Instead, she met with them as a group for an hour after school. In the discussion, she provided many good examples of how plagiarism inhibits intellectual growth; she talked about honesty and its relevance to scholarship and learning in school, about the value of authoring one's ideas, and about the competing value of sharing and building on one another's ideas as part of doing historical work. She required Sonia, Nikki and Paula to rewrite their reports, and Avi was told to write an essay about what she had learned from this experience.

Whereas Marie felt good about her decision and action in the end, her colleague across the hall with whom she had discussed the case criticized her decision, saying it was too lenient and not in line with the school rules. In this instance, Marie was confident in her action choice. Acting as she saw fit took courage, however, given the strong and vocal opinion of her veteran colleagues and professional friends, who held a different view. Nevertheless, with the courage of her conviction, she stood by her choice and met with the girls. At the time of this writing, she had received two of the new essays and was waiting for the other two.

❖ DOING TEACHING'S MORAL WORK

Marie's story reveals to us the moral nature of teaching and the challenge of teaching in a morally responsible way. Had we not explored her dilemma closely, we might have overlooked both the complexity of her decision to meet with her students about the plagiarism incident in her class and at the same time this aspect of the process of attending to the growth of these students as learning and knowing citizens of the world. We might have overlooked the inherently moral nature of teaching and the ubiquitous presence of moral reasoning required of teachers day to day. Looking closely and with care at the details of our work helps us realize the moral content of our work and why it matters in profoundly important ways.

Most teachers enter the profession because they want to "make a difference" in the lives of children they teach and, consequently, make a difference in the lives of the children's families and communities. The goal of making a difference in children's lives brings to the forefront the moral nature of teaching. When asked why they chose to teach, it is common for teachers to reveal deeply felt and often morally motivated reasons for entering the profession. In conversations I have had with teachers—both novice and veteran—we spend considerable time exploring what it means to make a difference in a child's life or what it means to be a "good" teacher or a "caring" one. Many teachers I know enter the profession with a "social conscience," Mary Kennedy (1990) argues for in the *Handbook of Research on Teacher Education,* but they don't arrive at teaching with what Bergen (1992) calls the "moral vocabulary" needed to reason through moral dilemmas so that they can engage in intentional moral action. For this reason, learning to grapple with the moral nature of the work of teaching is an important part of learning to teach. It is one part of the learning work of teaching that lasts a lifetime. Opportunities to share the deliberative processes involved in doing teaching's moral work help teachers learn to be thoughtful in productive ways, ways that make the daunting task of moral action more reachable.

❖ LEARNING AND MORAL ACTION

Learning in teaching is the keystone for moral action, not only learning that happens in preservice teacher education but also learning that lasts throughout the teacher's career. Learning from experience. Learning from talking with others. Learning from thinking deeply about one's actions as a teacher and the consequences of those actions for the students in one's charge.

Teachers do not arrive in the profession knowing how different actions will impact different kids, even if they arrive professionally well prepared. Rather, they use what they know upon entering the field to build a growing base of knowledge over a lifetime. If teachers aim to act in the best interest of children—which is at the heart of moral practice—and the children's world is constantly changing in complex ways, learning in teaching becomes the essential ingredient in doing their work well (Darling-Hammond & McLaughlin, 1995; Fullan, 1993; Hargreaves, 1994; McLaughlin, 1998). We can see how when one teacher engages in the thoughtful learning of moral practice, that extends person by person to the wider world of teachers, children, and schools. Responsible teachers respond to the changing context in which they work; as the children and their world change, so too must the teachers change, and as the teachers change, the schools that house them must change as well. At this juncture, then, a teacher's professional responsibility for engaging a change agenda intersects with the moral imperative of teaching all children well.

❖ CONCLUDING THOUGHTS

The idea of "teaching all children well" suggests the coupled themes of equity and diversity, which together provide the thread connecting the different chapters of this book. We begin our exploration of the principles with the moral nature of teaching because it provides a foundation on which the other principles rest. It also provides the core belief leading to our ultimate goal of teaching for an equitable, just, and more humane world. Given the demographic shifts of the last several decades, which have changed the complexion of American classrooms drastically, we are challenged more than ever in our goal of "teaching all children well." Yet, teaching all children well is exactly what we must continue to strive to do. The work is extraordinarily complex. Not only do children learn in different ways and have different needs, but those needs shift and change over time, just as the society around them shifts and changes. In this disequilibrating context, teachers must also grow and change if they are to meet the needs of the students they teach.

Learning in teaching is part of the moral responsibility of the work. An important piece of the learning agenda is to constantly question one's purposes in teaching and the consequences of one's actions: Do all students in my class have equal access to the learning opportunities I offer? As I look at the outcomes of my teaching, which students are achieving, and are there predictably students who are not? What happens when I consistently call on one group of students, and others remain silent in my class? Knowing how to frame questions like these and how to pursue answers to those questions are both important skills that teachers must develop over time. The questions rest on a base of professional knowledge that is also important for teachers to acquire as they continuously learn in their professional work.

As teachers, we must all work to better understand the moral dimensions of our work, which take into account both the purposes and the consequences of our actions. As a profession, we need to constantly evaluate how our work impacts the lives of the children we serve, their parents, their community, and our democracy. To "teach all children well," we must learn to recognize and name the moral content of our work and to grapple with the moral complexity we face in reasoning through the dilemmas that the realities of classroom and school life bring our way. The work is broad and encompassing, typically broader and more encompassing than we thought when we entered the field. A novice teacher with whom I worked describes what many of us have felt:

> I have really learned that there is so much more to teaching than imparting knowledge. If you had asked me before . . . to answer this question (what does teaching as a moral enterprise mean?), I probably would have postulated on the need for teachers to be moral beings within their own lives in order to be able to "show students the way." Now I have learned that morality is more than the modeling of moral behavior. I have an obligation to my students not only to model moral behavior but also to create a moral space in a world that is often not.

For this teacher and those who are her colleagues across this nation, the challenges of teaching in morally responsible ways are many. We must support the practice of teachers who work under the most challenging of circumstances to act in ways they believe are in the best interest of the children they serve. In that way, we all will be contributing to the making of a world that is more equitable, more humane, and more just.

❖ REFERENCES

Ball, D., & Cohen, D. (1999). Developing practice, developing practitioners. In L. Darling-Hammond & G. Sykes (Eds.), *Teaching as the learning profession* (pp. 3–32). San Francisco: Jossey-Bass.

Bergen, T. (1992). Teaching the art of living: Lessons learned from a study of teacher education. In F. K. Oser, J. L. Patry, & A. Dick (Eds.), *Effective and responsible teaching: The new synthesis* (pp. 346–364). San Francisco: Jossey-Bass.

Cuban, L. (2001). *How can I fix it? Finding solutions and managing dilemmas.* New York: Teachers College Press.

Darling-Hammond, L., & McLaughlin, M. W. (1995, April). Policies that support professional development in an era of reform. *Phi Delta Kappan,* pp. 597–604.

Fullan, M. G. (1993). Why teachers must become change agents. *Educational Leadership, 50*(6), 12–17.

Hargreaves, A. (1994). *Changing teachers, changing times: Teachers' work and culture in the postmodern age.* New York: Teachers College Press.

Hawkins, D. (1974). I, thou, and it. In *The informed vision: Essays on learning and human nature* (pp. 48–62). New York: Dyathon.

Kennedy, M. (1990). Choosing a goal for professional education. In W. R. Houston (Ed.), *Handbook of research on teacher education: A project of the Association of Teacher Educators* (pp. 813–825). New York: Macmillan.

Lampert, M. (1985). How do teachers manage to teach? Perspectives on problems of practice. *Harvard Educational Review, 55*(2), 178–194.

McDonald, J. (1992). *Teaching: Making sense of an uncertain craft.* New York: Teachers College Press.

McLaughlin, M. W. (1998). Listening and learning from the field: Tales of policy implementation and situated practice. In A. Hargreaves, A. Lieberman, M. Fullan, & D. Hopkins (Eds.) *The international handbook of educational change* (Part 1, pp. 70–84). Dordrecht, The Netherlands: Kluwer.

3

Preparing and Supporting the Reflective Practitioner

David M. Donahue

❖　❖　❖

> Dear Stern,
>
> Thanks for giving all the supplies that we need. With out you help is nothing like it because we need your help to provide us things that we need. Ms. Cramer + Ms. Tobin are happy that you gave us these things. also I appreciate what you had done for us hope some one would help you with what you want and what you need.
>
> Also once again thanks for what you give to us.
>
> Sincerely,
> Michelle Jones

AUTHOR'S NOTE: All the names used in this chapter are pseudonyms. Excerpts reprinted with permission.

Thank you

Dr. Stern

You are the man for giving us supplal to this 8th grade science class with out you this class would not had had no pencils or paper and stuff like that so I really apeat your help with or supples thank you.

Dear Dr. Stern

I wuld lik to say thank you for auplying all thise net mutirole's that wuld help or clasroom.

By Zack Taylor

Dear Dr. Stern

Thank you for giveing us the things we need for our class room. If it wasn't for you we would not have the thengs to luern with. . . . We will all use and appriciate the suppies every day in tell we live the school and the other studens that come will appriciate the suppies and were very happy that we have the things to luren with. and have fun with.

Thank you!

Sincerely,
Sheila Charles

Stacy was not sure what she should have done with these letters. At the time, she was student teaching in an eighth-grade science class at a middle school in Oakland. The school had recently received a gift from a local philanthropist to buy materials and equipment for science instruction, and Stacy's principal asked for a thank-you letter written by each of the students in the class to their benefactor. Stacy gave little thought to what seemed like a simple request, thinking the students would write for 10 minutes in class while she wrote her own cover note. After she collected the letters, she planned to put them in an envelope, send them off, and return to her science lesson. When she saw what the students wrote, she reconsidered this "simple" request.

She had sent the letters, unconvinced that she could teach all the grammar that needed revising and the spelling that needed correcting. She also wanted to move on with her science curriculum. Maybe the benefactor wouldn't really care about the letters. After all, the students were only eighth graders, and he might excuse the mistakes.

On the other hand, Stacy had conflicting feelings about her decision. It seemed more like a rationalization than a careful deliberation. A central tenet of her teacher education—that all teachers, regardless of subject area, are teachers of reading and writing—was starting to influence her thinking. As Stacy thought about writing in the context of her class, she realized that she needed to know more than techniques for teaching writing. As her colleagues pointed out, she also needed to know what her students already knew about writing in different genres, from lab reports to thank-you notes; about their experience with language, including Standard English; and about why they made the mistakes they did. In addition, she realized the letters raised questions of culture and power. Was it OK that a student wrote, "You are the man"? What did her students know about the language used by a retired European-American doctor? What would the benefactor know about the language used by African-American teenagers? Whose language should be used in the letters? When is it appropriate to require Standard English? What role does learning to write Standard English play in helping students gain and use power? How is the language her students use connected to their sense of identity? And why should her students be writing these letters in the first place? Why should they be "grateful" for paper and pencils when students in wealthier, suburban districts never give a thought to the source of money for basic supplies?

These questions and concerns demonstrate how Stacy's initial question—what should I have done with these letters?—was an opportunity for reflection on a number of topics through a variety of analytical lenses. Reflection, the principle on which we focus in this chapter, is closely connected to this book's other principles. After all, teachers reflect on something, and the content of their reflection may focus on subject matter or the political and moral contexts of teaching. Stacy's case illustrates all three: the role of writing in science classrooms, issues of power in language use and instruction, and the moral imperative of teachers to respect students' identity and give them access to power. Teachers also reflect on what their students know and should know, an idea related to learning as a constructivist and developmental process. Stacy's questions about her students' writing skills demonstrate this concern. The process of reflection illustrates another principle: collegiality. Whereas one image of reflection is the scholar alone with his or her thoughts, reflection can also be a social activity. In this case, Stacy's colleagues played a key part in helping her see new questions and reframe old ones with new perspectives. In the rest of this chapter, we discuss the nature of reflection, the need for reflection by teachers, its role in teacher learning and development, the tools that support reflection, and obstacles to reflection, including reflection in an environment of increasing regulation and high-stakes testing.

❖ THE NATURE OF REFLECTION

As you read the literature on learning to teach, you will find widespread support for the notion of teacher reflection. You will also find that educators mean different things when they refer to reflection. The collection of definitions can seem confusing and even contradictory. Some teachers conceive reflection as any thinking by a teacher, arguing that it is impossible to teach without thinking, and, therefore, it is impossible to be an unreflective teacher. At the other end of a spectrum of definitions, some teachers equate reflection with research, whether positivist, university-based investigations or teacher-action research. Our definition of reflection avoids these two poles. Instead, like many educators concerned with teacher learning and development, we base our definition of reflection on Dewey. In *How We Think* (1910), he called reflection the "active, persistent, and careful consideration of any belief or supposed form of knowledge in the light of the grounds that support it, and the further conclusions to which it tends" (p. 6). In the case that opens this chapter, Stacy was demonstrating persistent and careful consideration by bringing her questions about the letters to her colleagues and by continuing to examine her belief that teaching writing was beyond the scope of her science class. She and her colleagues brought multiple perspectives to bear on what role writing plays in the instruction of all teachers and the implications of these ideas for their practice, another prerequisite for reflection according to Dewey. When you reflect on your own teaching, ask whether the thinking you call reflection is active, persistent, and careful. Are you challenging your core beliefs and questioning what you know? Are you willing to examine the assumptions on which your beliefs rest, and are you willing to change those beliefs and the teaching practices based on them if those assumptions turn out to be unwarranted? When you are open to such questions and change in your practice, then your thinking can be called reflection.

In defining reflection, theorists have wrestled with questions of why teachers reflect, what they reflect about, and how they reflect. According to Dewey (1910), teachers reflect because they face a surprise, problem, dilemma, or puzzle that calls into question something they thought they already knew. More recently, Schön (1983, 1987) has also underscored the role of dilemmas in spurring reflection, in what he calls "reflection *in* action" at the time the dilemma is raised and "reflection *on* action" later, when the teacher revisits the dilemma. With its many unknowns, teaching is full of puzzling situations that promote reflection. In some cases, teachers recognize these puzzles on their own. In other cases, administrators, supervisors, mentors, or colleagues point out the dilemmas that prompt reflection. Stacy, for example, was taken aback by her students' thank-you letters, expecting them to be able to write in Standard English and finding out otherwise. Her colleagues also helped to identify other ways of framing her dilemmas.

Dewey (1910) locates the reason for reflection in puzzles and predicaments, and so those problems become not only the motivation but also the content for reflection. The problems may be located in a teacher's current practice (What do I do with these letters?), in past experience (What have students learned about writing?), or in future concerns (How will I create a science curriculum that integrates instruction in reading and writing?). Not only do problems differ in time orientation, they differ in type. Van Manen (1977) categorizes these problems into three different levels: practical/technical, social/political, and moral/ethical. For many teachers, reflection begins at the practical level, choosing from different means to achieve a known end. Consider Stacy's original question about what to do with the thank-you letters. Her concern also involved technical questions about how to teach Standard English. Reflecting with colleagues, however, Stacy also came to examine social and political questions as well as moral and ethical ones.

All teachers face a number of puzzles or dilemmas that call for reflection. Trying to make sense of the enormous content of reflection as part of a teacher's education, Zeichner and Liston (1996) identify five "traditions" of reflection—academic, social efficiency, developmentalist, social reconstructionist, and generic—each with a different purpose and focus. The academic tradition stresses teacher thinking about subject matter and is concerned with student learning. The social efficiency tradition emphasizes reflection on the extent to which one's teaching is in line with research findings and ways in which those findings can be put to use in the classroom. The developmentalist tradition focuses teachers' reflection on students' thinking and understanding. The social reconstructionist tradition assumes teaching is a political act, and reflection focuses on social conditions and teaching that lead to a more just society. Unlike these other traditions, the generic tradition, the most recent one to emerge, argues for the benefits of teacher reflection without specific concern for the topic of teachers' reflection.

When teacher reflection is based on the six principles described in this book, it cuts across the first four traditions. Stacy's case prompted reflection on academic questions about the place of writing in science classrooms and how students learn Standard English. It also connected to the social efficiency tradition, as Stacy and her colleagues discussed how different theorists and researchers would have responded to the problem. As she and her colleagues considered appropriate expectations for eighth graders, they engaged in reflection in the developmentalist tradition. Questions about the connections between language and power illustrated reflection in the social reconstructionist tradition. As you reflect on your practice, do not worry about categorizing your questions. Indeed, as Stacy's dilemma illustrates, reflection resists neat categories. Do think about these traditions, however, to avoid one simple way of reflecting on puzzles in your practice.

The Need for Reflection by Teachers

While some policymakers, textbook publishers, parents, and perhaps even teachers think of teaching as merely a technical activity of implementing curriculum according to established criteria, most teachers appreciate that teaching is intellectual work and reflection is a vital means of nurturing the intellectual dimension of teaching. Giroux (1988) describes the centrality of reflection in teachers' intellectual and political work, writing, "Teachers combine reflection and action in the interest of empowering students with the skills and knowledge needed to address injustices and to be critical actors committed to developing a world free of oppression and exploitation" (p. xxxiv). Thinking about students—what they already know, what they need to know, how they learn—is at the core of teachers' practice. It is not something teachers do only when problems present themselves in classrooms. Rather, it is a disposition toward thoughtfulness and inquiry that characterizes the relationship of teachers to students. When teachers believe their work requires thoughtfulness, they are more likely to create opportunities for student learning that require thoughtfulness. In such classrooms, teaching is based on student learning. Too often, people mistakenly believe that learning follows from teaching. As anyone who has been a teacher for any length of time knows, however, teaching a body of content or specific facts does not mean that students have learned that body of content or specific facts.

For those of us who believe that teaching is a political act, reflection changes the nature of relationships between teachers and students, leveling the playing field between the two. Reflective teachers do not remain in sole control of knowledge. In reflective teachers' classrooms, students are not the only ones gaining knowledge. Instead, students and teachers together create new knowledge about what, how, and why students learn. The classroom becomes more democratic, what Moll and Greenberg (1990) describe as a "fund of knowledge" in which no one member of a community knows everything, each member needs what others know, and each member contributes to the development of others' new knowledge.

Reflection allows teachers to become theory builders. Perhaps you have already heard about the split between theory and practice in teacher education. You may have even experienced this split: when a teacher tells you to forget everything you learn in your education courses because really learning how to teach happens in the field or when a professor intimates that the ideas of teachers who have not read the latest in critical theory or cognitive development should not be trusted. This split results from the persistent and mistaken belief that knowledge about teaching is created solely by "experts"; that is, researchers who devote their full time to conducting experiments to determine empirically "what works." In such a world, the role of teachers is reduced to implementing the findings of such experts.

We believe that knowledge about teaching is not created only by such experts and that teachers' roles extend well beyond implementing what others tell them works best "on average" in experimental situations. We believe that in addition to implementing the ideas from others' theories, teachers create their own theories. Such theory building happens through reflection. When teachers reflect on their practice, they are asking questions, forming hypotheses, and collecting data to answer their questions through a variety of means, from observing their students in class to examining their written work. They examine data to look for patterns: Do students complete more work during a certain unit compared to another?, for example. Teachers then use this analysis to develop findings, which may be additional questions for reflection. For example, if students complete more work during the unit on the Civil Rights Movement than on the Vietnam war, is that because they connected differently to the content because the units were taught differently, or because one unit was taught at the end of a marking period when students were concerned about their grade?

Ultimately, teaching is also hopeful work, and reflection plays a vital role in maintaining a hopeful stance toward teaching. When teachers ask questions, when they inquire into their own practice and into their students' learning, they are demonstrating their faith in their own learning. They refuse to give in to despair. In effect, reflective teachers are saying that what they do really matters, which is why they ask questions rather than teach in rote and formulaic ways. Annette, a teacher of several years, found reflection and inquiry gave her "an approach to dealing with all that I do with optimism and possibility— rather than bitching in the lunchroom, I ask questions, I wonder. I'm often frustrated but I do love that there are questions rather than stereotypes and rancor." For teachers like Annette, reflection provides a means to avoid the cynicism and despair that characterize teachers who have burned out. Developing a reflective, inquiring stance at the outset of your career is perhaps one of the best ways to retain the optimism and sense of hope that brought all of us to the profession in the first place.

Good Questions and Strategies for Teacher Reflection

Although reflection is important to sustaining thoughtful teachers, it is no panacea. For reflection to nurture the intellectual side of teaching, foster a sense of democracy in the classroom, and provide a sense of hope, teachers' inquiry must be based on important questions, questions where knowing the answer would make a real difference in what, how, or why you teach. We have all heard a teacher say at one time or another in our lives that "there are no bad questions"; still, some questions are better than others in terms of promoting useful teacher reflection.

The best questions focus on student learning, not teacher practice. For example, "how do students read instructions for chemistry lab?" is a better question than "how do I write instructions for chemistry labs?" or "how do I get students to read instructions for chemistry labs?" The last two questions put implications before findings. In other words, to know how to write instructions or to assist students in reading them you first must know what goes on in students' minds, what they know, how they learn, and what is confusing for them. The latter two questions focus on teachers as people who only act, rather than people who reflect and then base their actions on what they deduce from their reflection. The latter two questions about teaching practice also imply that one best way exists to teach all students and that the goal of teacher learning is to find that strategy. By contrast, questions about student learning are more likely to honor students' different ways of acquiring knowledge. As you develop your own agenda of questions about student learning, think about the students who will be the focus of your reflection. Are they the entire third-period science class? girls in advanced science courses? the students who sit silently in class and never say a word or hand in a paper?

As you formulate your questions to focus on specific students and their thinking, learning, experiences, and beliefs, you will find yourself moving from a teacher-centered way of thinking about a classroom to a student-centered one. As a consequence, students will seem less likely to have problems needing fixing and more likely to have valuable knowledge that will make a difference in your teaching. Viewing students this way will require you to collaborate with them as you collect data from them to answer your questions.

Tara, a student teacher in an urban public high school, provides a case of how to frame reflection as a new teacher. An English teacher who cares about helping students improve their writing, she asked how students interpret teacher feedback on final drafts of papers. Not only did the question matter to her because of her overarching goals as an English teacher, it was especially relevant as she found herself faced with stacks of papers to read and grade. Describing her inquiry, she wrote,

I found myself questioning the purpose and usefulness of my comments. On the one hand, I wanted my students to be aware of the mistakes they had made, but on the other hand, I didn't want to spend hours making corrections that would not be used for future writing.

Essentially, I wanted to know what types of comments were the most helpful for students to learn from. Also, if a multitude of comments are written, which ones do students read and why?

In a way similar to how Stacy framed her dilemma at the opening of this chapter, Tara is questioning her beliefs and knowledge. She is also leaving herself open to change in her practice as a result of her reflection.

To answer these questions, Tara engaged in a small action-research project. She asked her students to complete a short questionnaire asking:

- What are your first impressions of the teacher's comments on your papers?
- Do you read all the comments? In what order?
- Which comments are most helpful?
- Which are not helpful?
- What do you do with your paper when you get it back?
- How would you complete the following, "From the comments on my paper, I learned . . ."

By taking action to answer her questions, Tara learned that "most students *did* read all the comments," although she found their motivation for doing so varied. "Some read the comments because they were searching for explanations for their 'low' grades, and some because they wanted to know what they 'did wrong.'" She found that it was not the length of a comment "but how I phrase it that matters" to students, with short, explicit comments being the most helpful, according to students. She found that no students offered any comment on the extensive summary comments she wrote at the end of their essays, nor did any students remark on the positive comments she made. "What stood out was that students wanted to know when they made a mechanical error by having me mark it *every time*." Tara concluded her analysis and implications of the findings by writing:

I originally questioned [marking all errors] because I thought I would be bombarding students with negative feedback. However, their responses showed me they did care about being corrected, and doing so must be done in a way that is brief and explicit. And although no students cited the positive comments as being helpful, a few students wrote "thank you," and one wrote, "I like how you criticize my comments as to where it doesn't sound like my parents talking to me." I have learned that it is OK to mark every single mistake, as long as those mistakes are treated as learning events and coupled with thoughtful feedback about content as well.

Tara's inquiry resembles the type of reflection seen in experienced teachers. While many new teachers focus on their performance and their actions in front of a classroom, teachers with more experience typically ask questions about student learning. Good reflection requires more than anecdotal evidence, although such evidence may be the beginning of reflection. Thoughtful, purposeful data collection is more in line with our conception of reflection. In this case, Tara went beyond wondering what the looks on students' faces meant when she handed back papers. She asked students directly. Surveys and questionnaires are a useful and efficient way to collect information from a number of students. Sometimes, your questions for reflection have to do with the meaning students make or attach to various resources, events, or practices in the classroom. In such cases, providing students with a text provides richer data for your inquiry. For example, rather than asking students how their minds work when they read a history book, try asking them to "think aloud" as they read a selection from the book you use in class. A "think aloud" asks students to describe what is going on in their mind as they read. Another form of text might be a video. Instead of asking students what they think about participating in cooperative groups, ask them to join you in watching a video of them during cooperative group work during class. As you watch the video together, you can ask them why they did or did not talk or contribute to the group.

As you think about your own questions for reflection, try following some of the same steps Tara followed with her questions. Is your question about your practice or about student learning? If it is about practice, can you reformulate it so you're reflecting on student learning and its consequent implications for your practice? Can you describe why this question is important, why answering it really matters for how you teach? Can you think of active, persistent, and careful ways to collect information that sheds light on your question? As you engage in steps like these, you will move from merely wondering about something (always a good place to start reflection) to more sophisticated thinking.

Conversation and Writing Support Reflection

What does reflection look like? Reflection is an active process, but capturing an internal mental process is no easy task. Certain external conditions, however, can foster and display that internal process; namely, conversation and writing. In this section, we illustrate what reflection in conversation and writing does—and does not—look like. Not all teacher talk or writing is reflection. Consider the following conversation in a seminar class where new teachers are talking about their practice. As you read, think about what does or does not make this conversation reflective.

Abby: Today was my first week of teaching 10th-grade English, and I already have a situation that's made me unsure about what to do. I wrote a letter introducing myself to the students, telling them about how I came to California, what my experiences in school had been like, what my dreams for the future were, and what I like to do when I'm not teaching or taking classes. It was an honest letter, and I shared some of my pleasant memories of childhood and my hopes as a teacher with discouraging memories of being a high school student and struggling with prejudice against immigrants to the United States. I asked them to write a letter back to me, saying they could tell me anything and that if they weren't sure what to write about, they could look at my letter for ideas of topics. One student, Armand, a quiet young African-American man, wrote, "I hate school. I hate everything about it. All I want to do is burn it down." And he included a drawing of the front of the school going up in flames. Honestly, I don't know what to do, now. I said I would respond to each of their letters, but I don't know what I'm going to say.

Nora: You need to report this to the school administration. Schools are taking threats of violence very seriously these days. Who knows, he might really burn the school down, and someone could get hurt. Whether we like it or not, we have to take these threats seriously.

Kaitlyn: I'm wondering where his anger comes from. I think you should find out if there are any resources at the school or in the district for anger management or conflict resolution.

Sally: I would talk to him and tell him that you're concerned about his feelings about school. I'd tell him that we all get frustrated in our lives over various things at different times, but we have to control our feelings and find a way to keep going with our lives and not let anger or hate take over.

Carol: You know, this reminds me of a student I had several years ago. He was on medication to deal with a mental illness, but he stopped taking the medicine. I knew about the medication because I had seen a note in his cumulative file. When he started talking more and more about violence, I reported it to his counselor and we found out that he wasn't taking the meds.

Paul: That's interesting because this boy reminds me of one of my students. He's really into Goth, and he's always talking about death, destruction, and all kinds of depressing topics. I think it's really about the music and popular culture. We really need to help kids deconstruct that, take a critical lens to popular culture. I also think we can give them other, more positive images.

Tom: Sometimes, I think we make too big a deal about this kind of thing. I mean, when I was in high school, I was fascinated by video games, movies, and music with pretty violent themes. I'm kind of embarrassed about it now when I look back. But, I outgrew that fascination, and I think Armand probably could, too. I did all kinds of things, from drugs to fighting, as a teenager that I could have gotten in trouble for, but I've left that behind. I think we have to be careful not to make too much of what teenagers do and say.

Thinking about this conversation, would you say it was a reflective one? On the one hand, the teachers were talking about a real dilemma, and they had no shortage of ideas about what to do. Armand's letter definitely sparked a wide variety of responses from a group of concerned teachers. On the other hand, the teachers in this seminar tried to solve the problem before they talked about what that problem might be. Interestingly, Abby started the conversation in this direction by asking her colleagues about what she should do, rather than what they thought might be going on. Asked what she should do, they were more than able to come up with a list of actions. Abby's request about what to do is a common one among teachers. We are expected to act and to act quickly. Taking the time to reflect on how to frame a dilemma can feel like a luxury when decisions need to be made quickly, as was Abby's case, with its potential for violence. We have no illusions about the imperative for teachers to act, and we would not label these teachers' ideas as bad. What we would caution against is jumping to solutions to a problem before framing a problem. Even in a conversation like this where no single solution is offered, Abby is left with nothing but a smorgasbord of possible solutions, none explicitly tied to a theory about what was happening with Armand and what teachers should do. At the very least, however, this example illustrates one of the benefits of reflection through conversation: gaining many different perspectives. While it is not clear any of the individual teachers contributing to their conversation considered more than one perspective, Abby comes away from this discussion with a number of different ways to look at the dilemma she shared.

Returning to Dewey's (1910) definition of reflection as "active, persistent, and careful," we offer some suggestions about how this conversation might have been more reflective. Although reflection is active, it does not mean rushing to act or jumping to conclusions. Thoughtful, reflective action requires careful consideration of how to frame a problem. As the conversation above unfolded, we could assume that the teachers had implicitly framed the problem; for example, suggesting that Abby talk to the administration because they framed this as a case of potential school violence. We would suggest, however, that teachers ask themselves not only what is going on but also why; not only what they should do, but also why they should do it. In this sense, active means not merely taking action but taking the extra steps to interrogate one's thinking, to challenge one's assumptions.

Reflection is persistent or long-term in terms of scope of thinking and continually re-evaluating new information. Although persistent reflection occurs over the course of what we hope will be a career lasting years, persistence applies to situations that require quick decision making, as well. In such cases, teachers demonstrate persistence by grappling with different facets to vexing dilemmas and by turning over and over for several times an emerging idea as it evolves. Such persistence requires stamina in reflection. In reflective conversation, teachers can demonstrate reflection by thinking about responding not only to immediate dilemmas but also to other dilemmas or problems that may be created down the road as a result of making a change. None of the teachers in the conversation above took a long-term view. For example, what would be the outcome for Armand if the teacher went directly to the administration? What would be his future at school? What would be the outcome for other students in school who see students referred to an administrator as a result of their response to a school assignment? In the long run, how would you as a teacher reconcile allowing students free rein of expression with being concerned for school safety in an increasingly violent world? Reflective teachers demonstrate persistence when they consider several responses to dilemmas rather than clinging to one option. They continue to think about their response after implementing it rather than seeing their problem as solved. As time passes, reflective teachers continue to attend to new information that helps them re-examine their initial thinking and decisions about a problem. They realize that conclusions that "work" now for some may not work in the future or for all. Reflecting on such concerns, you may find yourself raising questions that will lead to a teacher research agenda over the course of years.

Finally, as Dewey (1910) points out, reflection is careful. Teachers who reflect with care recognize the complex nature of problems and bring various perspectives to problems. The conversation described above included a number of perspectives, but there is no evidence that the teacher incorporated them in thinking about a response to the dilemma. A good facilitator would help teachers think about where their perspectives on the dilemma come from, would challenge assumptions about the framing of the dilemma, and would ask for evidence that supports one framing over another. A good facilitator would also ask teachers to consider what perspectives are missing or what the limitations of their own perspectives are. For example, no one asked Tom to think about whether his own experience is a good basis for thinking about Armand. As a white man, Tom probably would not have been treated the same way by the school or justice system as Armand, an African-American man, for using drugs or talking about violence. How should a student's race influence how teachers talk to students about issues such as drugs? No one raised this aspect of the dilemma, whether because they were afraid of introducing race as a factor in the conversation or because they did not see it as relevant. As you engage in reflective conversation with colleagues, we encourage you to do so carefully, considering multiple points of view and explicitly considering how race, class, and other aspects of who you and your students are shape how you frame your reflection.

Just as talking can capture and nurture reflection, so can writing. The following excerpts from Ruby's student-teaching journal, to which her cooperating teacher, Sheila, responded, illustrate several aspects of what makes teacher writing reflective, including good questions rooted in practice and dialogue provided by a colleague's response. In one entry, Ruby wrote:

> Planning for the *To Kill a Mockingbird* unit is coming along . . . You showed me how you plan units (with the "into," "through," etc.), but how do you plan day by day? I find myself trying to stay aligned with the students' nightly reading (more or less), but then I realized that we didn't really do that for *Romeo and Juliet*. Is it more important to get through the major themes, or should class time relate in some noticeable way to the material that the students have just read? What's your opinion about this?

This excerpt highlights one important aspect of reflection: It raises questions. In this case, Ruby raises what might at first seem like a technical question: to align instruction with the students' nightly reading or to build from the nightly reading in different ways. But such a question raises larger issues about the purpose of curriculum, as Sheila's reply indicates:

> Balancing the day to day is interesting. I try to keep it tied to the essential question as best I can and other essential enduring ideas. Sometimes I'm right with the reading schedule; sometimes I'm not. You need to decide—what is important to me and the learning of these kids? . . . They don't need to understand every last little plot twist . . . , they need to grasp big ideas and important skills. Just say, what will they have with them in 20 to 30 years? It's not the plot! It is critical thinking. The literature is an inroad to awakening their analytic skills.

Sheila's response shows that few questions in teaching are purely technical, meaning that there is no single right answer for all situations at all times. Sheila's thinking illustrates the importance of purpose. What do you, as a teacher, want students to learn? Thinking about the answer to that question makes answering questions about how to align instruction with nightly reading a lot easier and makes clear that there is no single answer. For example, a teacher preparing her students for a test on the plot of canonical works might decide that, in fact, she does want students to remember plot and that her daily instruction should reinforce what students have most recently read. A teacher more in line with Sheila's thinking would align instruction differently. In any case, Sheila's reply makes us see the importance of raising the question, "why am I asking that," about all dilemmas for reflection.

On another occasion, Ruby wrote about her dependence on a limited repertoire of teaching strategies during her unit on *Romeo and Juliet*, raising questions with which many new teachers can identify.

I'm worried that my approach is too discussion-heavy and too teacher-dependent. For instance . . . , Did I really need to go over the balcony scene in the way I did? We talked about it a lot, but they hardly took any notes. How could I have approached my planning differently? I usually keep the goal in mind—and get there—but is my route effective, and how do I know it is?

Sheila responded, "You've got me thinking because sometimes it's so automatic, and automaticity at some level can be dangerous because it can lead to complacency. Why do we do things the way we do them?" Again, Ruby might be starting with a technical question about how to teach something in her classroom, but these questions almost always beg the question, why are we teaching something? With her years of experience, Sheila realizes that it's easy to fall into a trap of acting automatically. Although many new teachers might long for the day when much of their work seems automatic, Sheila sees the continued need to reflect, so she never falls into the trap of teaching something in a certain way because she's always taught that content in that way. To avoid that trap, she frames her questions for reflection not so much around how she will do something but around why she is doing something.

Both of the examples from Ruby's student-teaching journal reveal the social aspects of reflection and how it is situated in concrete contexts. Too often, we think of reflection as a solo activity, something that teachers do when they find time alone and when they tune out all the distractions of their classroom and the world. In fact, the best reflection often occurs when we have a colleague with whom we can frame our questions, consider other points of view on dilemmas, and examine possible responses. Again, the best reflection most often happens when we refer to a concrete situation. When we think about teaching in the abstract, we develop ideas that may only work in the abstract. Although such thinking can have value, the real world of teachers' practice is too full of particularities—about students, schools, goals, and prior situations, to name a few—to ignore in reflection.

Reflection in an Era of Regulation and High-Stakes Testing

Increasingly, teachers work under regulation and high-stakes testing of students and teachers. When teachers' work becomes more regulated, it also becomes "de-skilled," meaning teachers are not expected to draw on their own skills and ability to think. Rather, they are expected to follow guidelines and implement curriculum and policies made by others. In such an environment, reflection becomes much harder but just as necessary.

Of course, teachers have never operated with complete independence, and, despite the isolation of teachers in schools, they have never made decisions entirely on their own. We do not want to pretend that teachers ever enjoyed golden days of complete autonomy or that teachers should act without any oversight. After all, public school teachers work for the public and follow policies made by those working for the public. As a consequence, teachers have used district-approved textbooks, taught toward state and district expectations for subject matter at various grade levels, and followed government rules on everything from reporting suspected child abuse to including students with disabilities in the classroom. In the past, and in some places in the present, teachers have also been responsible for teaching values such as respect for the U.S. Constitution and appreciation of free-market capitalism.

What makes past practices of regulation different from the present? We believe the level of control and the attachment of high-stakes tests to those controls separate current regulation from the past. Although past efforts at regulation told teachers what to do, they left how to do it to teachers' determination, believing that teachers would know their individual students best. Also, previous regulations rarely spelled out in such lengthy detail what teachers were to teach. In the last 10 years, we have seen state frameworks in California in subjects like English and math nearly double in size.

For example, when teachers used district-approved textbooks, they made decisions about how to use them. If history textbooks provided one perspective on the past, teachers might supplement those with texts providing other perspectives and ask students to put the different perspectives in conversation with each other. A science teacher might use a textbook's description of the solar system to pose open-ended questions beyond the facts recounted in the narrative. An elementary school teacher might choose to start somewhere other than in the beginning of a basal reader, depending on the skills and readiness of her students. Much of the current regulation harkens to an earlier era of "teacher-proofing" curriculum in the mid-20th century. As they do today, policymakers of that time believed the nation was in crisis—a Cold War at home and abroad then, struggling for position in a global marketplace today—and that schools were part of the solution. Professors from leading universities developed curricula in science, math, social studies, and foreign language that supposedly would not rely on teachers' skills for success. Yet, teachers still made decisions about how to implement this curriculum, picking and choosing certain lessons, blending new curriculum with old.

Today, teachers are expected to teach toward tests, many of which assess knowledge at the factual level and many of which are norm-referenced, meaning a student's performance is compared to that of other students taking the test rather than to criteria for satisfactory achievement. Norm-referenced tests ensure that 50% of all students will always be at the "bottom" in terms of achievement. Attached to these tests are high stakes for students—graduation from high school and placement in mainstream classes—and high stakes for schools—extra money for improvement, reconstitution for failure. To prepare students to do well on tests, school districts have invested in curriculum packages geared toward tested subject-matter content and skills. Teachers are judged by how well they implement the curriculum according to directions, leaving less room for teachers to make decisions about modifications for individual students and classes.

At first, regulation and testing might seem to reduce the need for reflection. After all, what is there to think about when teachers are told what to teach and how to teach it? As you may know from considering questions about managing to teach all that is considered important in various standards documents, grading students according to standards, or maintaining a sense of professional identity when being so closely regulated, the need for reflection has not disappeared. The only things to have changed are the questions for our reflection. Given the dilemmas of standards and testing, what are some the questions that come to your mind for reflection? What follows are three sets of questions for reflection that we see arising from such dilemmas.

The first set comes out of the desire all teachers have to see their students do well, to make sure that no doors to opportunity are closed to them. These include questions such as:

- How do I teach all the standards that are deemed important when I have less than enough time?
- How do I engage students in learning standards-based content and skills?
- How do I prepare students for tests that will have a large impact on their lives?

These questions reflect our wish to succeed as teachers and to have our students succeed in the public school system as it currently exists. They focus on how to teach rather than on what students know or why something is important because many of the standards handed down to teachers and the tests tied to those standards obviate the need for teachers to think about what students know or why content is important. Content is important because it is tested. What students already know is not necessarily the beginning place for building curriculum in such an environment; rather, the standards documents themselves are the starting place. Notice how these questions stand in contrast to our description earlier of good questions for reflection, questions that focus first on student learning rather than on teaching.

A second set of questions reflects the desire of teachers to reimagine schools, to interrogate the assumptions underlying standards tied to high-stakes testing. These include:

- Why is the content of high-stakes tests valued?
- How do high-stakes tests affect my students' learning and their opportunities after school?
- Who benefits and who loses in a world of schools shaped by high-stakes testing?
- In what ways, if any, are standards and tests fair measures of students' learning?

These questions come from teachers' attention to reconstructionist traditions in reflection, from their understanding that teaching is inherently a moral and political endeavor. They come from a belief that schools routinely and predictably fail some students and that schools do not always have to be the way they are now.

The third set of questions results when teachers necessarily try to balance two worlds: the world of schools as they are, with their high-stakes tests, and the world of schools as they might be, with learning measured in a variety of ways and with no punishment attached to assessment. These questions are:

- How do high-stakes tests affect my students' learning?
- What do my students value and know about the content set forth in standards documents?
- Based on the answer to the previous question, how do I design a curriculum to help my students meet those standards?
- How do I work in a way that meets the obligations set out for me by the state while still remaining true to the values I hold?
- How does my role as a teacher concerned about students' learning extend beyond the classroom level to policies at the school, district, state, and federal level?
- How do I prepare students to gain broad literacy skills, participate in democratic life, engage in productive work, and lead a meaningful and fulfilling life?

Like the productive questions for reflection described earlier in this chapter, the answers to these questions really matter. They are complex and without easy answers. They call for multiple perspectives. Also, they are too big for any teacher to face alone. We hope you will engage your colleagues in reflective writing and conversation to examine these questions and to develop new questions in response to the particular context where you teach.

❖ REFERENCES

Dewey, J. (1910). *How we think.* New York: Heath.

Giroux, H. (1988). *Teachers as intellectuals: Toward a critical pedagogy of learning.* Granby, MA: Bergin & Garvey.

Moll, L., & Greenberg, J. (1990). Creating zones of possibilities: Combining social contexts for instruction. In L. Moll (Ed.), *Vygotsky and education* (pp. 319–348). Cambridge, UK: Cambridge University Press.

Schön, D. A. (1983). *The reflective practitioner.* New York: Basic Books.

Schön, D. A. (1987). *Educating the reflective practitioner.* San Francisco: Jossey-Bass.

Van Manen, M. (1977). Linking ways of knowing with ways of being practical. *Curriculum Inquiry, 6,* 205–228.

Zeichner, K., & Liston, D. (1996). *Reflective teaching: An introduction.* Mahwah, NJ: Lawrence Erlbaum.

4

Constructivism in Teacher Education

Rethinking How We Teach Teachers

Linda R. Kroll

A s Professor Plum, Sarah examined her cards, her *Clue*[1] game sheet, and her opponents' positions before making a final accusation. She was sure of the cards in the envelope in the center of the board. "Aha!" she exclaimed, "I'm sure I'm right."

"How do you know?" asked her partner, Naomi, who was a novice to *Clue*. Using her *Clue* sheet, Sarah demonstrated which of her opponents surely had certain cards, which cards she had, and which cards she thought her opponents had. She based her conclusions on her own suppositions, her observations of her opponents' suppositions, and general sneaky *Clue* strategies that she had employed as she played.

AUTHOR'S NOTE: All the names used in this chapter are pseudonyms.

Naomi was interested and somewhat confused as she struggled to understand the logic of the game and Sarah's game-playing strategies.

Sarah and Naomi were members of a class for preservice teachers and educators in development and learning where, for this class period, we were playing the board game *Clue* to practice analyzing the task demands of the game and simultaneously to understand the different ways that people play the game. This activity simulated, in many ways, what teachers have to do all the time: analyze what the lesson they are teaching requires students to understand and, at the same time, make sense of what their students are actually doing with the lesson. If the teacher's analysis has been accurate, then, by comparing it to what students are doing, they can figure out the most effective ways to help those students who are conceiving of the lesson differently than they had envisioned. On the other hand, if teachers do not really understand the cognitive demands of the lesson in the first place, then, when their students do not understand, teachers will have difficulty figuring out what else they might do to help them.

Thinking about teaching and learning in this coordinated way is based on a particular theory about how people learn or acquire knowledge—the theory of constructivism. Constructivism is not a theory about how to teach, but it helps inform our teaching. It reminds us that the learner must be at the center as we think about our curriculum, our subject matter, and our pedagogy. In addition, constructivism does not define learning as simply the acquisition of more and more knowledge. Rather, learning is a developmental process that results in qualitatively different ways of thinking about the world as we grow; learning is one kind of development. Thus, understanding both the nature of the learning process and the paths of development provides teachers with a basis for understanding their students' needs and strengths.

We believe that all teachers need to learn about constructivism and developmental theory and to teach in a way that recognizes that people construct their own knowledge and that this construction process is a developmental one. This dual focus on constructivism and development results in a pedagogical dilemma for teacher educators, a dilemma with which we are continually grappling and with which we know that you as teachers will ultimately grapple: the dilemma of what to teach and how to teach it.

The first part of the dilemma is what do teachers need to know about constructivism and developmental theory? This is, in many ways, a subject matter dilemma, much like what do teachers need to know about history or mathematics? There is no one correct definition of constructivism; in fact, its lack of definition has led to many misunderstandings of what constructivism is and is not, among them the notion that constructivism is a way of teaching (which we maintain it is not). Ernst von Glasersfeld (1996) describes how constructivism is different from other theories of cognition:

> What we call knowledge does not and cannot have the purpose of producing representations of an independent reality, but instead has an adaptive function. This changed assessment of cognitive activity entails an irrevocable break with the generally accepted epistemological tradition of Western civilization, according to which the knower must strive to attain a picture of the real world. (p. 6)

In other words, knowledge is developed as a result of adaptive behavior on the part of the knower, rather than the knower developing a model of true knowledge or ultimate truth. Such a differentiation is so different from our commonsense notion about the nature of knowledge and learning, especially as most of us have experienced it in American schools, that constructing such a differentiation for oneself is a developing process that requires time. In addition, knowledge is not constructed alone. Human beings are social beings. They live and work together. Knowledge construction itself, as an adaptive behavior, is also done in the context of a social milieu. Whether the construction occurs *actually* in company with others, or in interaction with tools constructed by others, or in interaction with one's environment, it is never done alone.

The second part of the dilemma resides in the belief that to learn something, people must construct their own ideas. This is how you learn; thus, no matter how you are taught about constructivism, what you come to know about constructivism is a result of your own construction process. Even if you are taught in a way that does not reflect a constructivist view of learning (e.g., being asked to memorize formulas or definitions and examples), you still construct some sort of understanding. In addition, this construction process does not occur in a vacuum; rather, it is the result of your struggle with what you read, what you hear from your peers and your teacher, how you relate what you read and hear with what you see in the classroom, and what you do in learning and teaching. What I choose as a teacher to have you read, what I tell you during class time, what activities I ask you to do, and how I help you reflect on what you have done—and the personal effort you use to put all these things together so that you make some kind of coherent sense—all of this contributes to your individual understandings of constructivism and the way people learn. My goal as a teacher is that my understanding and your understanding will concur or overlap. I cannot directly pass on to you my own understanding of constructivism. Thus, I have to teach in a way that not only will allow you to construct an understanding but will truly support that construction process.

In this chapter, I am going to reflect on this dual dilemma. First, I will talk about what and why you should learn about the theory of constructivism and developmental theory, including what it is I hope you come away with from your own teacher education experience. This is the *what* aspect of the dilemma. Second, I will talk about how we can apply these ideas across different aspects of teaching, including pedagogical questions, curriculum, and issues of establishing safe, supportive learning communities. I will share some actual instances of reconstruction with regard to how our preservice teachers understand their own learning of subject matter, particularly with regard to literacy. This is the *how* part of the dilemma. All in all, I will try to show you how the principle of learning as a constructivist/developmental process is fundamental to learning to teach.

❖ A BRIEF DEFINITION OF CONSTRUCTIVISM

Before continuing, however, it seems to me that it is both necessary and helpful to have a common definition of constructivism, at least for the purpose of this discussion. As stated, constructivism is a theory about learning and about how people "get" knowledge. Embedded in this theory is a concept of what knowledge is and what it means to have it or to get it. As Fosnot (1996) states, constructivism is a "theory (which) describes knowledge as *temporary, developmental, nonobjective, internally constructed, and socially and culturally mediated.*" Learning (or how we "get" knowledge)

> is viewed as *a self-regulatory process* of struggling with the conflict between existing personal models of the world and discrepant new insights, constructing new representations and models of reality as a human meaning-making venture with culturally developed tools

and symbols, and further negotiating such meaning through cooperative social activity, discourse, and debate. (Fosnot, 1996, p. ix, my italics)

What does it mean to say that *knowledge is temporary and developmental*? In constructivist theory, knowledge is constantly changing as learners reconstruct their understanding of a particular phenomenon. Thus, it is both temporary, in the sense that there is no "once you know something, that's it!", and developmental, in the sense that your knowledge is constantly changing—we hope toward greater understanding by putting together the ideas that go together and sorting out those things that initially seem the same but, in fact, work more effectively when they are found to be different. *Knowledge is nonobjective, internally constructed, and socially and culturally mediated.* Knowledge is not a picture of an independent reality. Rather, what you know is a result of your acting on the environment, using what you already know to understand new information and to incorporate this new information into your already existing schemes of knowledge. Such incorporation often requires a restructuring of your own schemes, thus resulting in new and more complex schemes. This *self-regulatory process* is an act of balancing your current knowledge with new insights that may or may not conflict with that knowledge. This act of internal construction is supported and guided not only by an individual's internal structures but also by the social and cultural context in which people find themselves. Your social and cultural context interprets and influences your interaction with the world through, among other things, language, customs, technology, and history. This notion of the importance of cultural context expands our view of what it means to interact with the environment and demonstrates the power of social interaction as part of that environment.

❖ TEACHING ABOUT CONSTRUCTIVISM AND DEVELOPMENTAL THEORY

Teachers need to understand how to use developmental theory to think about their practice in an ongoing and practical way. It is not enough to be able to identify the stages of development or the processes of behavior management that are associated with positive and negative reinforcement. Rather, developmental theory must help teachers to understand how children learn, how individual children's learning may differ, and, particularly, how they learn particular subject matter. Thus, teachers must pay attention to the evidence of development in their students' understanding through both the right answers they give and the wrong. Teachers must learn to investigate the thinking behind their students' answers and not to assume that because a student gives a particular answer, he or she understands the problem in a particular way.

While preservice teachers will construct their own ideas about constructivism, certain basic elements to the theory seem essential to making good use of the theory. The first basic idea is that children's thinking and understanding is not simply less developed than adult understanding; it is qualitatively different. Learning is not simply an additive process but requires reconstructing and restructuring at every level. A first entry into this understanding of qualitative differences is becoming familiar with Piaget's descriptive stages of development (Piaget & Inhelder, 1966/1969). It is convenient to explain the notion of five year olds struggling with number sense by saying the child is "in the preoperational stage of development." It is convenient to have a label to hang your hat on but, ultimately, not particularly helpful. However, it is helpful to pay attention to general characteristics of thinking and problem-solving behavior. As preservice teachers begin to generalize about what characterizes the thinking processes of young children, they are able to notice how these thinking characteristics show up, not only in Piaget's experimental tasks but also in school-learning activities. Thus, one content-learning goal about constructivism for beginning teachers is to know and recognize the ways of thinking that are characteristic of the various stages of development.

For example, four to seven year olds tend to focus on one aspect of a problem rather than coordinating more than one aspect, and thus, they tend to be led by perceptual rather than logical aspects of a problem. Such thinking is often quite adaptive because things are *often* what they seem. For example, *usually,* a longer line of objects has more objects in it. However, you can't just pay attention to the length of the line; you also have to notice the size of the spaces between the objects. So there are two aspects of the problem to consider: line length and space between objects. Younger children tend to focus only on the length of the line. What children still have to do is to sort out which aspects of a problem have consequences for solving the problem and which do not. While such *centration* may dominate the thinking of young children, it does not entirely disappear as they get older. It is not unusual for adults, when confronted with an unfamiliar type of problem, to begin by focusing on one or two aspects to the neglect of other significant portions of the problem. Because this is something we all have a tendency to do in *unfamiliar* territory, as teachers of *familiar* territory it behooves us to investigate what the children we are teaching focus on and what they are neglecting. As teachers, too, we tend to relate new issues to things we already know. We use already well-established means to address new problems. It is only through repeated reflection on the viability of what we have done that we develop new means and strategies to solve problems that may seem old, but for which we have perhaps developed a new perspective through the reflective inquiry process.

A second aspect of developmental and constructivist theory that teachers need to construct is how to figure out what it is children are thinking about a problem. As you come to realize that you cannot simply tell children what they don't know, you need to develop techniques for figuring out what children do know and build on that knowledge. This requires that you understand what the children *need to know* and what they *do know,* not just what they don't know. As in the *Clue* game, teachers need to analyze the problem they are investigating to determine the kinds of understanding and knowledge the problem requires. Then, they need to be able to find out what the children understand about the problem and what question the children are answering as they solve the problem. The notion of "what question they are answering" goes to the heart of the child's conception of the problem. If the teacher can understand what the child knows and how he or she is applying that knowledge, then the teacher can begin to think about how to teach the child. By practicing Piagetian tasks,[2] participating in adult versions of Piagetian and school-learning tasks, and creating tasks out of school curricula, you can begin to develop questioning techniques and ways of thinking about children's learning that allow you insight into children's ways of thinking about school-learning tasks. Ultimately, teachers can learn to use a version of Piaget's experimental *clinical method* or *method of critical exploration,* both to assess how their own students are understanding and learning the material they are trying to teach and to determine what to teach next. This is what Naomi was doing when she questioned Sarah about her *Clue* solution. Earlier in the game, she questioned Sarah about her strategy for finding the solution. Each time Sarah made a "suggestion,"

Naomi asked her why she'd chosen these particular clues and how she hoped that would help her solve the mystery. When Sarah raised strategy issues regarding confusing her opponents, as well as solving the mystery, Naomi realized that Sarah was considering several aspects of game playing: identifying the cards in the envelope by figuring out which cards her opponents did and didn't have, confusing her opponents as to which cards she had, and winning the game by solving the mystery first.

As teachers become more experienced, they develop ideas about how children learn the subject matter they are being taught. Applying critical exploration techniques to understand the development of subject matter content can greatly aid teachers in developing new curriculum and applying prescribed curriculum to teach subject matter content. Thus, the better teachers understand both the misconceptions and accurate but incomplete conceptions that children tend to develop along the way to understanding, the better they will be able to teach. For example, in teaching punctuation, if a teacher understands what a child is thinking about the use of the period (early on a child may believe that the period appears at the end of every line), then he or she can build on that child's incomplete understanding of what the period is used for in writing. But knowing how to make sense of what the child is doing requires the teacher to step back from easy assumptions about what is happening and to investigate through clinical questioning what the child is doing. Thus, teachers must form hypotheses, conduct observations, develop possible questions, test out these questions with their students, form some conclusions, and then standardize the way they ask students about particular issues while continuing to allow for the personalization that the clinical method provides (Cowan, 1978). There are ways to help beginning teachers to learn this process.

When preservice teachers are asked to replicate Piagetian tasks with a few children, analyze the results, and attempt to draw conclusions about children's levels of cognitive development, they begin to understand how to use the clinical method. The activities, questions, and possible follow-up activities and questions have been laid out for them almost like a recipe. Thus, they can compare the results they get when they practice with what Piaget and Inhelder (1948/1967) found in their own research. However, when teachers are asked to select school-learning tasks, analyze the understanding required to succeed (the cognitive demands), develop and use a protocol[3] for investigating particular children's understanding, and draw conclusions about the children's understanding of the content, then they are really beginning to connect development, constructivism, and teaching. You might imagine something you have taught recently and think about how you would question children to see *how* they understood what you thought you had taught. This is not easy to do, and, as in all learning, there are steps toward greater understanding along the way.

When you begin to analyze school-learning tasks you may find that you are mostly able to relate the task to cognitive developmental levels (i.e., did the task require sensorimotor, preoperational, concrete operational, or formal operational ways of thinking?). Again, it is useful to have a label for what you think you have learned; although labels can also be limiting. Thus, you might equate age with stage, which, although it is a beginning of understanding, does not get at the qualitative differences between stages.

In devising and analyzing their own school-related problems, many preservice teachers move beyond the age-equals-stage understanding. In a kindergarten classroom, Carolina examined the children's understanding of a chart related to the calendar that was used to figure out how many days they had been in school. The original chart was arranged in rows of 10. Each time the children entered a day on the calendar, they added one day to this chart positioned directly below the calendar. Carolina hypothesized that, given different chart arrangements of days (like 1 row out of 3 rows of 10 compared to 2 rows out of 4 rows of 5), children would be deceived by either the length or the number of rows rather than focus on the number of squares making up each row. Such a response is typical of a child who does not understand number conservation. Carolina wondered if

> by being able to see in front of them the number of days represented by cards with increasing number symbols, are the children truly understanding number progression, or are they simply learning the language of counting, memorizing the proper order of numbers . . . unaware of the meaning of numbers and the significance of quantity?

She related the problem of understanding the "How many days have we been in school chart?" to failing "to conceptualize logically that changes in appearance, such as physical rearrangement or dimension, may be irrelevant and may not affect quantity." She predicted that her 5 year olds would respond at Stage 2 of preoperational thinking, that they would use one-to-one correspondence or counting when comparing the charts, but that they would be inconsistent in their ability to compare the different arrangements. She predicted that they would focus on one aspect of the problem and that their thinking would be dominated by the perceptual aspects of the problem. This is a good analysis of what the task's cognitive demands might be, and it shows that Carolina is beginning to construct for herself what number conservation or its lack may look like in a classroom activity.

Once teachers have analyzed the potential cognitive demands of a task, they have to devise a protocol for checking out their students' understanding of the task and see what strategies those students use for solving the problem. Two issues arise in this endeavor: First is aligning the protocol of questions and activities with the cognitive demands of the content, such that you are really asking the child to solve the problem you are interested in; second is interpreting what you find and learning to follow the lead of the child as you individualize the subsequent questions. The clinical method requires that you be attuned both to your subject matter and to the student's thinking. Keeping track of both requires lots of practice. (Piaget mentions that to become good at the clinical method requires a year of daily practice.) Sometimes, preservice teachers have an "aha!" moment in the process of questioning their students. When Melanie investigated the understanding of ratio in three of her students in her fifth- and sixth-grade placement, her delight in the responses and her own understanding was palpable. Her interpretation of the results (which were really classic—in that two out of the three understood the 1/2 ratio in a number of circumstances, whereas the third child recognized that the smaller measurement tool required more "scoops" but had no idea of how much more) indicated her understanding of what she was seeing. She commented on the usefulness of this procedure: "I love how Piaget's highly intellectual propositions can come to life and be accessible and important in our daily thinking and doing (in the classroom)."

On the other hand, preservice teachers often have difficulty interpreting what they see, although these difficulties often highlight their initial difficulty in planning a task to assess what they want to assess. That is, the task you design to investigate the reasoning of your students must in fact require that they use the reasoning you are investigating. Thus, Anne reported on children's performance on a division and multiplication task. Her question was how the children understood the reversible relationship between multiplication and division. She used a problem they had been doing in class and developed questions she thought would help her understand the children's notions about the relationship between multiplication and division. The children who were successful with her task were the ones who could *name* the relationships between multiplication and division problems such as $30 \div 5 = 6$, $30 \div 6 = 5$, $5 \times 6 = 30$, and so on. If children could *say* these problems, then Anne assumed that they understood the reversible relationship between the equations. She suggested to the children that they use manipulatives if they wanted, but she did not ask them to use the manipulatives to demonstrate what they meant. Thus, she really had no way of knowing, from what the children did, if their understanding was the result of strong rote learning or a concept of the relationship between multiplication and division. In Anne's reflection on the results of her task experiment, she indicated that she might have been making some unsupported assumptions about what the children understood.

> I was looking to see if the children could reverse their thinking and make connections between division and multiplication, but I think I only tested to see if they could do this in an abstract way. Although I gave them all the option of using the chips, I don't know if it was clear how the chips could be used for this purpose.

What Anne probably meant here by *abstract* is *verbal*. The children were able to say the relationship between a set of equations, but relating those equations to one another does not really demonstrate an operational understanding of the reciprocal relationship between multiplication and division. If she had required them to show her with the chips what they meant, she would have gotten a better idea of how they saw the relationship of putting things in groups to add them more efficiently (multiplication) to putting things in groups to subtract them more efficiently (division). As it was, Anne really had no idea how they understood the relationships they were able to name. When teachers develop curriculum that aims at children developing deep understanding, then the teachers' questioning of the children must allow them to demonstrate the extent of their knowledge.

When preservice teachers are asked to apply the clinical method to school-based learning and then analyze the cognitive demands of the task, they tend to select mathematics or science to investigate. Applying Piagetian ideas to mathematics and science is more straightforward than seeking to apply these tasks to other areas of the curriculum. Sometimes, however, preservice teachers will venture into the unknown and investigate language, literature, or geography. Although this can be much more difficult, a thoughtful addressing of such problems allows them to extend their understanding of Piaget's ideas and the notion of constructivism into areas they have not yet considered. Jessica gave four different proverbs to three 7th-grade students (two of them English Language Learners [ELLs]) to see how they would interpret metaphorical language. She was investigating how the students might be comprehending text. She made the task more complicated for herself by selecting ELL students, but, nevertheless, she had some very interesting insights. Her first important insight was how literal two of the students' interpretations of the proverbs were. These students said things like "If you throw stones and you live in a glass house, the house might get cracked!" for the proverb, "People who live in glass houses shouldn't throw stones." The third student had a more inferential response, translating this proverb into a version of the golden rule. Jessica was surprised at the results, partly because she hadn't really known how to think about this task before she administered it. She recognized that there were developmental differences between the literal and inferential interpretations, but she did not feel she had an understanding of what might be at the root of these different ways of looking at the proverbs. She finished the task by feeling in great disequilibrium, but it seemed to me that she was beginning to see beyond the clinical tasks to the real curriculum. ELLs obviously might have more difficulty with metaphorical language, but even the native English speaker had difficulty making inferences.

Overall, beginning teachers, having experimented with applying the method of critical exploration to school-learning tasks, are convinced that developmental and constructivist theories offer insights into children's thinking and that they can, if they think hard enough about it, use Piaget's methodology to understand what their young students are learning as they teach. As Julia wrote at the end of her paper:

> Clinical interviews based on classroom curriculum are very effective ways at getting at children's levels of understanding because what they ask us to do is investigate behaviors that are already observable. These children and these tasks provided me with a window into preoperational thought and to a kind of assessment that seems fair to children.

Thus, Julia is beginning to understand how to get at children's understanding, but she continues to struggle with what it means to construct an understanding.

Playing *Clue* with a partner who uses clinical questioning to investigate a player's reasoning gives everyone the opportunity to try out all aspects of assessment, teaching, and theory application in the context of their own thinking and learning. As participants evaluate the different strategies used by different players, they discover that the more experienced players use a "control of variables" approach to eliminate possible cards and identify the true murderer, weapon, and location. They have learned about control of variables as one manifestation of formal reasoning identified by Piaget. As they see this in action, teachers come to better understand the possibilities inherent in many different activities for understanding children's thinking and developing their further reasoning abilities. They ask themselves, Why are they doing that, and what might they be thinking? We hope this continual reflection on the "why" of students' actions, along with speculation and investigation of "what" they may be thinking, will become a habit of mind.

However, it is one thing to pick one school-learning task and develop a protocol to investigate one or two children's understandings and another to develop curriculum and assessment that continually allows you to get at what your students are thinking as you teach. Preservice teachers have difficulty applying this specific knowledge to the curriculum classes where they are asked to assess children's understanding of mathematics and literacy and actually using it "on their feet" as they teach. While creating Piagetian-like assessments from school-learning tasks might lead them in the right direction, it is still not a straight path, and the difficulty of connecting constructivism and developmental theory to what they are going to teach is evident. Thus, a second part of learning about constructivism and developmental theory requires reconstructing your own knowledge about subject matter and finding places where you can apply the clinical method and your knowledge of children's developing understanding to your teaching.

❖ APPLYING CONSTRUCTIVIST THEORY TO
UNDERSTAND HOW CHILDREN LEARN CONTENT

In thinking about the application of constructivist theory to how to teach, you must make several steps. First, you must understand what construction of knowledge in that subject matter area might look like. What are the issues that require construction and reconstruction, and how does thinking in this subject relate to constructivism and developmental theory? Second, what does it feel like to construct knowledge in this subject matter? While you "know" literacy, mathematics, science, and social science, what it means to learn these contents is not something most of us have paid much attention to until we have to teach it. When you think about your own learning process, it can help you to understand your students' learning processes. Third, you must connect these two areas, to relate development within the content area to how one constructs knowledge within the content area at particular points of development. Thus, in learning to teach literacy, you not only learn how to teach children to read and write and use spoken language effectively, but you can simultaneously rediscover your own literacy learning process. This simultaneous construction of pedagogy and content can enable you to consider how to create a classroom environment for your own subsequent students that will allow for their construction of literacy.

This double journey begins with examining the developmental nature and path of learning to read and write. You can re-examine your own learning of literacy by writing a literacy autobiography, as do our students. These autobiographies serve four purposes. First, they help you reflect on the process of learning to read and write from a personal perspective. What can you remember of your own experience in becoming literate? Second, the autobiographies help you reflect on the process from a developmental perspective. Is what you experienced anything like the developmental process you read about in texts written by authors such as Holdaway (1979), Calkins (1994), Chall (1983), or Kroll (1998)? How? Third, when you do this with others, the sharing of the autobiographies can take you out of your own personal perspective to consider the plethora of experiences present in one classroom of 30 students. Beginning teachers generally have one of two perspectives going into this project. They think everyone learned to read and write the way they did (these are generally the successful readers and writers), or they think they are unique, in that no one else had such difficulties or pain in learning to read and write. The variety of reactions and experiences that they hear about in people's different experiences opens their minds and eyes to the variety of experiences their young students will have. It helps them to see that there is no one way that people learn to read and write. When beginning teachers understand that there are multiple paths to learning to read and write, they connect this understanding with the theoretical understanding that prior knowledge, culture, and social context affect the specific learning and development of an individual.

The fourth benefit of this project is that, when done with others in a particular framework, it can bring beginning teachers into the writers' workshop. The process of writing and rewriting the auto-biography is, for many, the first time they have written anything in which they have control over the form, the length, or the content. In addition, the autobiography is ungraded. This lack of the expected usual constraints makes many beginning teachers uncomfortable. It is a first disequilibrating step to rethinking their own literacy. Thus, within this project, they are thinking about the pedagogy of teaching reading and writing and at the same time rethinking their own literacy both past and present.

For our preservice teachers, the autobiography is the beginning of a framework for continued development in understanding the literacy learning process from personal, developmental, and pedagogical per-spectives. Whether the focus is on assessment, pedagogy, or content specifically, attention is often drawn to the other aspects, as well as to their own continual learning of literacy. In each activity and in each written assignment, participants can construct for themselves what this has to do with literacy learning and what the learning is. If you have similar opportunities, you will frequently have the chance to consider the construction of literacy from different perspectives. This reflection on the teaching of literacy can help you to formulate a stance on assess-ment, pedagogy, and content.

As you and other preservice teachers learn to teach literacy, you have to continually reconstruct your ideas about the learning of liter-acy. As you read further, try doing the following spelling activity. In thinking about the learning and teaching of spelling, you have to think about the content (what are some possible spelling patterns in English we haven't thought about?), the pedagogy (can discovery of spelling patterns help children learn to spell?), assessment (when would this be an appropriate pattern for children to examine?), and, finally, your own spelling knowledge. We all remember rules in spelling that hold most of the time. Remember the one that goes "*I* before *E* except after *C*, or when sounded like *ay* as in *neighbor* and *weigh*"? Even this rule has common exceptions like *height*. Take a look at the following spelling list of 25 words that end in *tion* or *sion*.

caution	nation
civilization	partition
conclusion	passion
creation	persuasion
faction	petition
fission	portion
fusion	position
fruition	possession
initiation	precision
invasion	variation
invitation	vision
motion	solution
motivation	

What patterns do you notice? Is there a rule? What resources did you use? If you are reading this text with others, check with them about what they thought.

We did this activity in our methodology class for the learning of literacy. The preservice teachers were asked to figure out if there was a rule or pattern for when to use *tion* or when to use *sion*. They immediately asked me "*Is* there a rule?" (looking to see if there is a "right" answer). They then proceeded to discuss the problem in small groups. When they were finished, they wrote their rules or patterns on the board. Each group came up with several observed patterns, which they called rules. Some were more consistent than others, but all indicated a careful examination of possible patterns. Janie and her colleagues proposed that there were usually slight differences in pronunciation between *tion,* which is pronounced /shən/, and *sion,* which is sometimes pronounced /zhən/. Except for *ss* configurations, this is a *pretty* consistent rule. "We don't always notice these subtle differences," said Janie, "but they help in thinking about spelling patterns."

Several groups noted that words ending in *tion* were usually words that could stand by themselves (fruit/fruition). Sometimes, you had to add an *e* at the end when you dropped the *tion* (initiate/initiation). They also pointed out, however, that this rule could often apply to the *sion* words, too. Kathy noticed that *nation* was another kind of exception.

"What if where it comes from, the word's origin, makes a difference?" Karen wondered. She got a dictionary but was then confused about how to tell from the entry what the word origin was. A group discussion led Tim, Alice, and Karen to discover that *L* in a definition means from Latin and *ME* in a definition means from Middle English. They found that all of the words on the list were originally from Latin roots, although some had come through Old French and some through Middle English.

These preservice teachers employed a variety of strategies in determining rules: adding other words to the list to verify that what they were seeing was true on a wider scale; using dictionaries to find related word families and origins; thinking of cases where the rule did not work. In debriefing the activity, several conclusions were reached. First, patterns can be recognized, but there is nothing that could really be called a rule. However, there were certainly differences in pronunciation that they had not first recognized. This is content knowledge about the English language spelling system. Second, encouraging children to systematically examine the spelling of English would give them productive strategies for figuring out how to spell words they are not sure how to spell; there are strategies for helping children learn to spell accurately that do not depend on brute memorization of lists of hundreds of words; rather, learning to spell, like many other aspects of literacy, can be a constructive process. Here is a pedagogical observation. Third, for those teachers for whom accurate and conventional spelling has always been a challenge, they suddenly saw that they could reconstruct their own understanding of English spelling patterns to improve their spelling accuracy (reflecting on their own literacy). For the purposes of becoming literate as a constructivist process, this last conclusion was in many ways the most important. By reflecting on their own construction process, these preservice teachers were able to construct new knowledge for themselves and reflect on the construction of literacy by the children they teach.

As our preservice teachers learn to think about pedagogy and content, they are also asked to consider how they will assess their students' understanding and learning and how they will teach based on these assessments. In learning about the teaching of literacy, they are given several assignments that require that they first focus on a child's literacy understanding and ability and then plan (and, we hope, teach) appropriate literacy instruction. They are asked to apply what they have learned about using the clinical method to understanding how children understand the reading and writing processes. They use a variety of appropriate "on your feet" assessment tasks that I suggest. These tasks are not unlike the ones they designed for the subject matter-assessment assignment discussed earlier, asking them to make use of their understanding of the clinical method to complete the assignment successfully.

Something that our preservice teachers try that you could also try is using a series of running records and miscue analyses to look quantitatively at one student's reading over time and to plan and teach to that student's needs. Taking running records is a technique used primarily by teachers of beginning readers to examine the strategies and techniques children use as they read aloud familiar and unfamiliar text. As children read aloud, the teacher marks all correct and incorrect renditions of text, including repetitions, guesses, and substitutions children use to read the text effectively (Clay, 1993a, 1993b).[4] Reading miscue analyses (RMA) are a more detailed and descriptive version of the running record, used primarily with older readers reading unfamiliar text. Again, it is used to note the reader's use of strategies, miscues, and understanding of written text (Goodman, Watson, & Burke, 1987). As our preservice teachers complete the last of these analyses, for many of them it is still a procedure that tells them about the child's reading, but it has not helped them to think about what to teach to help the child to move forward.

However, some of our beginning teachers have shown that they have begun to understand the interplay between assessment and teaching, that they see the miscue analysis as a version of the clinical method, and that they can see the children they are working with constructing new ideas about reading before their eyes. One student teacher was working with a group of fourth graders, all ELLs. The cooperating teacher required her to use a particular text, but when Susan used the text for a miscue analysis with one of the children, she discovered that it was much too difficult. The teacher insisted that she continue to use the text anyway. With great ingenuity, Susan designed several activities that would help the children read the text with understanding.

The text was about a boy detective. The language was full of plays on language and metaphorical language (or slang), which for ELL children could prove challenging. Susan designed a game that involved solving a mystery (so that the students played detective) by reading words that came out of the text in the context of the game. Susan described the success of one student as he danced back to his seat humming to himself, "I could read the words!" In creating her game, Susan recognized that the students needed both content knowledge and sight word recognition to read the text successfully. Based on her miscue analysis, she was able to design instruction that allowed the students to construct an understanding of detectives and to learn some of the words of the text.

Helen was working with a fourth grader who was reading well below grade level. After his first miscue analysis session, she concluded that he needed help in comprehension strategies. Subsequently, she taught four comprehension lessons to the whole class involving purpose for reading, prediction, inference, and cause and effect. She closely observed the child's participation in these lessons and was confident that he would do better on a second miscue analysis. In fact, she found that he did worse, although the text she gave him was slightly less difficult than the first text. She concluded that he was being asked to read texts that were much too difficult and that, therefore, he was not able to use independently the comprehension strategies he had practiced with the class. Her recommendation was to give him less difficult reading material so that he could improve his reading comprehension. Helen's analysis of a child's reading took her more than one session, but her reflection on what constitutes a good condition for learning to read is insightful. Her understanding that one cannot learn to read to understand from a text that is too difficult is an understanding many teachers could use.

Ultimately, I hope that you and our preservice teachers will understand how constructivist theory can help you to figure out how children become literate and how you can support this development and learning. Through participating yourself in literacy teaching practices based on a constructivist theory of learning, and through assessing and prescribing for the students you are teaching, I believe you can become able to construct for yourself a workable position on the teaching of literacy.

❖ COORDINATING CONSTRUCTION
   OF CONTENT KNOWLEDGE WITH
   CONSTRUCTION OF PEDAGOGICAL KNOWLEDGE

Each time we do an "adult" version of a problem our preservice teachers might use with their own students, they learn something more about their own learning process. Sometimes it is difficult to step back from the teacher role and examine the learner experience. But when they use both their own metacognitive abilities (to consider what they have constructed and how that has occurred) and the clinical method (to understand how their classmates are constructing their individual understandings), their whole concept of the teaching of that subject matter changes. We saw briefly at the beginning of this chapter how Naomi and Sarah had that experience in playing *Clue* as partners.

For our preservice teachers, there is nowhere that this metacognitive experience occurs more frequently or more strongly than in the ongoing writers' workshop[5] (Calkins, 1994; Graves, 1994), which they participate in during the spring semester. We begin the workshop with a writing session during the first week of the semester. We have about six additional sessions where we write for 30 to 45 minutes in class. I try to model a real writers' workshop, although there are built-in constraints that I indicate to them from the beginning, such as the lack of time, both in each session and in the number of opportunities they have to work in the workshop context. Nevertheless, by the third week they are beginning to behave like writers. They plan what they will work on in class; they think about their piece during the week and often work on it; they work on more than one piece at a time; they begin to conference with one another. There are always some who find the whole process terrifying. The variety of reactions to the workshop is important for discussion. While many people may be comfortable with trying on this role as a writer, imagine what it must be like if you are not. The writers' workshop makes public the process of learning to write. Those who are embarrassed by their lack of ability or comfort in writing are often compelled to confront this discomfort. Just as it is important for me to consider this for the preservice teachers who are my students, so is it important for you and other teachers to consider that it may be equally uncomfortable for some child or children in your own classrooms.

I attend most carefully to those beginning teachers for whom it is most difficult. If you are uncomfortable with a subject matter yourself, it will be difficult for you to teach it. Susan, who was in tears the first week or two, commented after the fifth week of writers' workshop (about 8 weeks into the semester) that in spite of her resistance, she had conferred with a classmate and found that she had written a lot and that what she had written was "not bad." On the other hand, Ellen, a beginning teacher who found other subject matter difficult, loved the writers' workshop and shared something she wrote during the workshop period, a simple observation piece filled with interesting imagery. Alice, who told me "she has a stomachache before every writers' workshop class," commented that when Ellen read her spontaneous piece, she (Alice) felt liberated. She no longer felt her piece had to be perfect and polished before she could share something. As the importance of their own writing is recognized, the preservice teachers feel more able to teach writing and to allow their students to have the opportunity to write and feel like writers. As Mary Ann, a student who graduated a number of years ago, wrote:

> Teaching seems to demand a journey of self-discovery . . . If students face continuous blocks in their writing, how can I help them unless I examine the blocks I encounter and try different approaches to break through? By understanding my own writing process, I might be better able to understand the process of writing for my students. Unless I am an active writer—experiencing the personal struggles and triumphs of writing—how can I sincerely, honestly help the students I teach? The thought of writing from a creative and personal place scares me. The struggle within me can be an asset, for with it I can understand the struggles of other writers.

In reconstructing your own notion of what it means to learn to write, you can begin to think about learning to write as a process of construction and reconstruction which you can share with your students and with which you can empathize.

❖ CONCLUSION

Constructivism is a theory about how people learn. In order for you as a beginning teacher to understand what this might mean, you have to consciously experience knowledge construction for yourself and to experiment with setting up opportunities for children to show you their own construction of knowledge. As teacher educators, we are constantly constructing and reconstructing ways for our preservice teachers to participate in these processes. For all of us, what to teach about constructivism, either as a theory of learning or as a way of thinking about the learning of a particular subject matter, and how to teach in a way that promotes preservice teachers' construction of subject matter, pedagogical, curricular, and learner knowledge is an ongoing fascinating challenge.

In order for you as a teacher to consider knowledge construction in a way that is useful to you in your teaching, you will have to continue to experience it consciously. You will want to ask yourself questions such as:

- How are my students learning particular subject matter?
- How are these students this year like or unlike the students I have taught before?
- How is what they bring to the classroom in the form of knowledge being drawn on in what I am asking them to do?
- How am I helping them to make use of the funds of knowledge they already possess?
- How am I building on what they know and can do?
- How am I finding out about this for each child?
- How am I changing as a teacher as I pay attention to how and what my students learn?

As you think more deeply about these issues, what and how you teach will change. Your teaching may come to reflect the developmental process your students are undergoing, and this, in turn, may change what your students do. It is an ongoing reciprocal process of learning and development on the part of both you as the teacher and your students.

Each of the principles highlights particular aspects of being a teacher. *Learning as a constructivist / developmental process* puts the focus on the learner: what the learner knows, what the learner brings with him or her from home and earlier experiences, what the learner understands, what question the learner is answering. Coordinating this focus with the other five principles is a complex process, which our preservice teachers are beginning to know how to do by the time they leave us. For us, as professors, this coordination is also a challenge. It is as if each principle can act as a camera lens on the act of teaching and what happens in classrooms, in schools, and in the greater learning community. A constructivist lens focuses on the child as learner. As Carmen said, in a tone of great discovery, "Constructivism is about learning, not about teaching!" This differentiation between learning and teaching is an important one for all teachers to make as they think about what and how they teach.

❖ NOTES

1. *Clue* is a board game published by Milton Bradley Co. in which anywhere from three to six players try to figure out who murdered Mr. Body, with what weapon, and in which room, using a deck of cards representing all the suspects, weapons, and rooms. The answer is contained in an envelope in the center of the board. For each game, new cards are selected and hidden in the envelope. Each player gets an equal number of cards and on her turn has the opportunity to "make a suggestion" about each of the clue categories (murderer, weapon, room). Players try to find out what other players have while concealing as much information as they can about their own holdings. Each player has a recording sheet to keep track of the information he or she learns. When players are sure they know, they make an "accusation" and are allowed to check the contents of the envelope. If they are right, they win the game.

Players employ different strategies to solve the problem. The most efficient strategies involve controlling variables. Thus, players may make a suggestion using two out of three cards that they hold in their hand. If no one shows the third card, they know which of the three cards they named is in the envelope. Likewise, if someone else makes a suggestion to which no one can respond, players using a control of variable strategy can use that information to discover which of those cards is in the envelope and which is held by the player in question.

2. One of the legacies of Piaget's work is his vast compendium of tasks that he used to investigate children's understanding of primarily mathematical and scientific reasoning. (See, for example, Inhelder & Piaget, 1964; Piaget, 1941/1965; Piaget & Inhelder, 1948/1967; Piaget, Inhelder, & Szeminska, 1981.) These tasks have been replicated with so many children that, in spite of the personalization of each administration of the task, they are highly reliable and replicable. Thus, beginning teachers can use these tasks to practice figuring out what children understand because the answers are pretty predictable. By analyzing both their questions and the children's answers, teachers can work on their own use of clinical questioning or the "method of critical exploration."

3. A protocol is a set of questions and activities, with possible follow-up questions and activities to understand a child's thinking with regard to a particular problem. Questions and activities used in the clinical questioning will ultimately be individualized for each child.

4. Running records are used primarily with younger readers and with somewhat familiar text. The goal is to see what strategies children use and how they use them in a particular difficulty level of text. Do they rely on phonics alone? Do they rely on context cues? Do they reread to clarify their understanding? Do they read with expression? How do they deal with miscues, or what seem to the skilled reader like mistakes? If they have too many miscues

(more than 10% of the text), then this text is too difficult for them to read or learn to read at this point in their reading learning.

5. For further information on writers' workshops, there are many resources, including those noted here. Briefly, a writers' workshop is a pedagogical context for teaching writing. The underlying philosophy is that children learn to write most effectively by behaving like writers from the beginning of the learning process. The workshop is designed to support them in many ways as they draw and write their way into authorship.

❖ REFERENCES

Calkins, L. M. (1994). *The art of teaching writing.* Portsmouth, NH: Heinemann.

Chall, J. S. (1983). *Stages of reading development.* New York: McGraw Hill.

Clay, M. M. (1993a). *An observation survey of early literacy achievement.* Portsmouth, NH: Heinemann.

Clay, M. M. (1993b). *Reading recovery: A guidebook for teachers in training.* Portsmouth, NH: Heinemann.

Cowan, P. (1978). *Piaget with feeling: Cognitive, social, and emotional dimensions.* New York: Holt, Rinehart & Winston.

Fosnot, C. T. (1996). *Constructivism: Theory, perspectives, and practice.* New York: Teachers College Press.

Goodman, Y. M., Watson, D. J., & Burke, C. L. (1987). *Reading miscue inventory: Alternative procedures.* New York: Richard C. Owen.

Graves, D. H. (1994). *A fresh look at writing.* Portsmouth, NH: Heinemann.

Holdaway, D. (1979). *The foundations of literacy.* Portsmouth, NH: Heinemann.

Inhelder, B., & Piaget, J. (1964). *The early growth of logic in the child.* New York: Norton Library.

Kroll, L. R. (1998). Cognitive principles applied to the development of literacy. In N. Lambert & B. McCombs (Eds.), *How students learn: Reforming schools through learner-centered education.* Washington DC: American Psychological Association.

Piaget, J. (1965). *The child's conception of number.* New York: Norton. (Original work published 1941)

Piaget, J., & Inhelder, B. (1967). *The child's conception of space.* New York: Norton. (Original work published 1948)

Piaget, J., & Inhelder, B. (1969). *The psychology of the child.* New York: Basic Books. (Original work published in 1966)

Piaget, J., Inhelder, B., & Szeminska, A. (1981). *The child's conception of geometry.* New York: Norton.

von Glasersfeld, E. (1996). Introduction: Aspects of constructivism. In C. T. Fosnot (Ed.) *Constructivism: Theory, perspectives, and practice* (pp. 3–7). New York: Teachers College Press.

5

Preparing to Teach Content

"Not Just a Series of Fun Activities"

Vicki Kubler LaBoskey

Four preservice teachers were discussing lessons they had recently observed their cooperating teachers teach. Their task was both to briefly describe the lessons to their peers and explain the reasons given for the subject matter content.

Beth: My cooperating teacher taught a lesson about frogs to her second graders. They had just finished studying butterflies, and she was now teaching frogs in a comparative way. She said she was doing so because one of the State of California life sciences standards for second grade says that they need to know that the sequential stages of life cycles are different for different animals.

AUTHOR'S NOTE: All the names used in this chapter are pseudonyms.

Hector: I am in a kindergarten classroom. Vivian, my cooperating teacher, is doing a unit on pumpkins, since Halloween is coming up. The lesson had to do with estimating the circumference. The children had to estimate how big around in inches their class pumpkin was, and then they measured it with a tape measure and compared the actual measurement with their estimates. She says she does it every year at this time; she likes to construct her units around themes related to kids' interests.

Crystal: My cooperating teachers—I have two of them who share a contract—taught a lesson to their eighth graders on bridge building with straws. The students worked in groups, and the aim was to try to build a bridge that would hold the most books. The teachers had gotten the idea from a workshop they attended and thought the kids would really enjoy it.

Francesca: My cooperating teacher taught a mini-lesson to our third-grade class on subject-verb agreement. She said she did so because she had noticed that many of them were making several mistakes with regard to that in their writing.

Even in these brief commentaries, we can see that there are a myriad of factors to be considered in lesson and unit planning. Furthermore, there are a number of different ways to proceed in making these decisions, the possible results of which are virtually limitless. How should you go about deciding what to teach? For the lesson? For the unit? For the year? What is it, if anything, that all first graders should know about writing, about mathematics? All 12th graders? Who should determine what knowledge matters? For which students? What does it mean to *know* physics? History? How do you tell whether or not a student understands the meaning of democracy? Or knows multiplication? Should you teach reading any differently than you teach art? To this student or to that student? In this context or that context?

These are some of the questions regarding subject matter that you should be asking yourselves on a regular basis when you prepare to teach content—a daunting list of complex queries that have been debated by subject matter specialists and other educators for centuries. Are some answers to these questions better than others? Are some approaches more viable? How can you decide? Where should you begin? Why does it matter?

❖ A PRINCIPLED APPROACH

It matters because the fundamental purpose of your work is to educate. Martin Haberman (2000) makes a distinction between *schools,* on the one hand, and *day camps* or *custodial centers* on the other. He argues that the former are places where teachers engage students in sustained and productive learning efforts. He critiques urban schools in particular for being more the latter than they should be, which is disastrous for the children who attend them:

> Serious learning requires sustained activity over days, weeks, and months. And much of that activity is unpleasant *work.* In the "schools" that youngsters in poverty attend, staff members are fixated on management and getting through each day. By themselves, there is nothing wrong with activities such as making a turkey from a paper bag or visiting a museum or viewing a video on Eskimos. But whether the activities have learning potential or are merely jejune time fillers is determined by the teacher's ability to generate sustained effort. The bits and pieces of disconnected things without any cumulative meaning that are typically offered to these youngsters do not meet the standard for learning in any recognized field of knowledge. (p. 207)

As a result, Haberman (2000) concludes, the students in urban schools end up not really knowing much of anything. But Howard Gardner (1991), in his book *The Unschooled Mind,* contends that the results are not more encouraging for any students anywhere.

In my work with elementary preservice teachers, I have characterized this all-too-frequent curricular problem as "just a series of fun activities." It occurs when individual lessons, although action packed and even content rich, remain just that: individual lessons. Not being guided by any overall subject matter goals and having no connections made between them, these experiences are of limited educational value; they do not help children become powerful knowers, either within or across disciplines. My colleagues at the secondary level often comment that the problem is not confined to elementary teaching.

Lessons for adolescents can be just as disconnected although not necessarily so enjoyable; thus, the comparable problem in high schools might be referred to as "just a series of not-so-fun activities."

Two of the lessons described at the outset might be in particular danger of falling into this trap. Although we would, of course, have to know much more about what was happening in each context over time to be able to tell for sure, certain factors should flag our attention. Most questionable is the kindergarten lesson on pumpkins, for two reasons. The first has to do with the nature of the curricular context in which this mathematics lesson is situated. Now, many teachers construct all or parts of their curriculum around themes, and there are many good reasons for doing so. The literature on educating English Language Learners (ELLs) (e.g., Freeman & Freeman, 2002; Peregoy & Boyle, 2001), as well as that derived from brain research (e.g., Kovalik, 1997), suggests that theme-based instruction can provide especially meaningful learning opportunities to students. However, the chances for constructing units that are "just a series of fun activities" can be heightened by this approach, calling for extra care in ensuring knowledge is developing over time, both within as well as across disciplines. A second problem to be attended to here is that the particular concept objectives—circumference and standard measurement—are probably not developmentally appropriate for this group of learners. If a teacher is attending more to the theme and the interest of an activity than to the subject matter, then the likelihood of youngsters engaging in exercises with no ultimate meaning for them is increased.

The other lesson that we would want to interrogate especially carefully with regard to this issue is the one on bridge building. Teachers get their ideas from many sources; for example, textbooks, workshops, the Internet, magazines, books, and colleagues. These can provide you with wonderful, significant lesson possibilities. In fact, this lesson has much potential for contributing to the students' understanding of science, mathematics, or even social studies, but only if the teacher helps to make those concepts explicit and connects this lesson to others that deal with relevant aspects of the subject matter(s). As Haberman (2000) pointed out, no matter how engaging or inherently valuable an activity, if it is not an integral part of a sustained learning effort, it is not educational.

A central aim of your teaching must be the development of powerful subject matter knowledge. Drawing on the work of Robert Moses (2001), Alan Schoenfeld (2002) argues that mathematical literacy is a civil-rights issue. What he means is that to gain access to higher education and well-paying jobs in this country, as well as to participate fully in the rights and responsibilities of citizenship, students, most particularly the poor and students of color, need to know mathematics. Similar arguments could be made for the other disciplines. There are, therefore, moral, ethical, and political reasons for helping your students construct serious in-depth disciplinary knowledge. This is what we mean by taking a "principled" approach to teaching when starting with a subject matter focus: You design and implement your curriculum and instruction so that all of your students can *construct* powerful *subject matter knowledge* for *ethical* and *political* reasons using a *reflective, collegial* process guided by *moral* reasoning and *an ethic of care*. But what might this mean in practice? How can you actually do this? Where might you begin? The remainder of this chapter will be devoted to the explication of a planning heuristic I have developed with the help of many cadres of credential candidates over the last several years. It is a tool for thinking and decision making that may or may not prove useful to you but should at least provide a concrete example of what principled planning might look like.

❖ A PRINCIPLED PLANNING HEURISTIC

These issues are complicated but can be particularly challenging for elementary teachers because they have to work with so many different disciplines, some of which may not be areas of substantive expertise. I will use elementary examples in this chapter, both because of that added complexity and because these are the people with whom I usually work. But the questions to be asked and answered are the same regardless of grade level and of whether or not you are teaching one or many subjects in California or Kansas. The proposed approach (see Figure 5.1) can work equally well for any teacher anywhere.

❖ THE DESCRIPTION

The heuristic is not a recipe; it is not formulaic. What it does do is make explicit the general factors to be considered in the planning process, as well as highlight some of the most pressing questions to be addressed. In addition, it illustrates the active and interactive nature of the

Figure 5.1   Heuristic for a Principled Planning Process

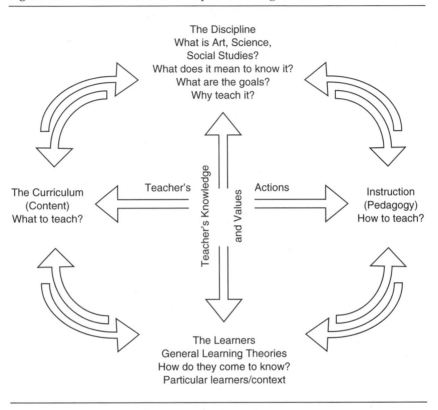

endeavor and its many potential starting points. First, I will explain the different aspects of the framework and then illustrate two of the several different ways you could use it to take a principled approach to curricular development and implementation.

The vertical axis has to do with what you as the teacher know and value—your theories of teaching and learning, if you will. The horizontal axis represents your planned curriculum and instruction, or what you actually choose to do in your practice. The circular presentation of these factors and the bidirectional arrows represent how all aspects interrelate with and impact one another. Furthermore, the figure is meant to suggest that this is a recursive, responsive process with no real beginning or end.

The top of the vertical axis, which could just as well be at the bottom, has to do with your knowledge and values regarding the subject matter you are teaching. It includes your definitions of the discipline, with what you consider to be, in Schwab's (1964) terms, both its substantive knowledge (what constitutes the content knowledge of the discipline) and its syntactic knowledge (how knowledge is generated and tested in the field). It involves conceptualizations of what it means to know and engage in the subject matter at different stages of development and of why that knowledge is important.

Fortunately, in constructing your perspectives on these matters you do not have to start from scratch; many resources are available for consultation. Of course, your state frameworks or standards will provide guidance in this regard; in fact, most states will require attention to, even compliance with, their formulations. The national subject matter organizations, such as the National Council of Teachers of Mathematics, the National Council of Teachers of English, the National Science Foundation, and the National Council for the Social Studies, to name a few, also have documents conceptualizing their disciplines and iterating appropriate standards. The National Board for Professional Teaching Standards, structured according to subject matter and school level specialization, can also provide an important perspective on these issues. The cataloging could go on, which in itself can be part of the problem. The differences between and among these various positions can sometimes be extreme; Suzanne Wilson (2003) has referred to this phenomenon as the "curriculum wars." How are you to choose which one or ones to follow? As the lists of standards proliferate, how are you to cover them all? Even if you do, there are no guarantees that powerful subject matter knowledge will be the result; the whole, as they say, is greater than the sum of its parts. So although the frog lesson may hold more promise for providing a worthwhile learning opportunity for the students because it is based on a state standard, you are still responsible for both evaluating the merits of that standard in the first place and, if you embrace it, helping your students make the necessary connections, something this teacher seems to be trying to do by making comparisons with previous work on butterflies. Many additional questions have to be asked and answered, and there is much that you need to know and consider.

Bottom line, to make these judgments you must have adequate knowledge of the discipline yourself. What is adequate? This is also a hotly debated topic in various educational arenas and one that we will not be able to answer here. Useful to our purposes, however, is work like that done in mathematics by Ball and Bass (2000), who suggest that what you need is "pedagogically useful" content knowledge. By that they mean, "Teachers need mathematical knowledge in ways that equip them to navigate . . . complex mathematical transactions flexibly and sensitively with diverse students in real lessons" (p. 94). You need to be able to "use subject matter knowledge to figure out what [your] students know, to pose questions, to evaluate and modify [your] textbooks wisely, to design instructional tasks, to manage class discussions, to explain curriculum to parents" (p. 99). It means not only that you need to be able to do the mathematics yourself but that you have the wherewithal to "hear students flexibly, represent ideas in multiple ways, connect content to contexts effectively, and think about things in ways other than [your] own" (p. 94). Again, Ball and Bass are speaking about mathematical knowledge in this case, but similar arguments are being made for other disciplines such as history (Wilson, 2001) and science (Driver, Asoko, Leach, Mortimer, & Scott, 1994).

Because knowing for teaching is different than discipline-based knowledge, substantial background, even expertise, in a subject matter will not guarantee that you know the content in ways that will enable you to teach it well to your students. Furthermore, scholars like Kevin Kumashiro (2001), interested in anti-oppressive education, suggest that the knowledge you have gained about social studies, English, mathematics, and science is very likely a "partial" story, representing the singular viewpoint of the dominant social group. You will thus need to "look beyond" what you already know and are being asked to teach in ways that can ensure more inclusive understandings. You need to be—and help your students learn to be—critics of the disciplines. Embracing this aim of change, Kumashiro states, will require you to become comfortable with uncertainty in your educational interactions with your students. You will have to accept that neither the outcomes nor the means for getting there can be fully specified ahead of time. It means your "lesson plans need space for the unpredictable and uncontrollable things that always get in the way of knowing [your] students and achieving [your] objectives" (p. 10). You will need to reflect on your lessons by asking not only, "What 'worked'?" but also, "What did this lesson make possible and impossible? In what ways did it enable repetition, crisis, change, and so forth?" (p. 10).

In essence, Kumashiro (2001) is suggesting that you can only know what and how you need to teach the disciplines in the context of actually attempting to do so, which is not unlike a position taken by Ball and Bass (2000). In our heuristic, this is represented by the center, where all of the various aspects come together in practice and reflection on that practice—where your knowledge and values with regard to the disciplines and the ways in which particular learners might come to know them are put into action. It is also where your actions can begin to feed back out to your knowledge base and your planning processes, but only if you reflect on them in thorough and thoughtful ways. One promising vehicle for facilitating such reflection, according to Ball and Bass among others, is the student work that results from these activities and interchanges, which directs our attention to the bottom of the vertical axis in the heuristic. This has to do with your theories of learning, as well as your knowledge of the particular learners you are teaching and the context in which you are teaching them.

One of the other chapters in this book, Chapter 4, should be particularly helpful to you with regard to this aspect. Again, you do not have to start from scratch; there are many available resources. As always, however, the ultimate responsibility is yours: You must decide what learning theories will guide your curricular decision making now and in the future. In addition, you need to continuously redecide based on new evidence and understandings, which by implication means you need to stay informed about them. What is critical is that those theories are well constructed, empirically justified, and socially responsible; they must be systematically formulated with an aim of ensuring that *all* learners will be able to develop powerful subject matter knowledge.

A virtually universal perspective in the field at present is that you must attend to your particular students when making decisions about the teaching of content, a rationale supported by both learning theory and political ideals. As stated by Lewis and Johnson (2002), "Classrooms characterized by post-modernity are open, the teacher and students share power, students are actively engaged in constructing their own knowledge, and learning is conceived of as a dialogical and social process" (p. 57). This means that students should have a voice in curricular decision making; their interests, values, and expressed needs will influence your teaching. In addition, it implies that you will have to take into account the multiple aspects of your student population and context; for example, race, gender, ethnicity, language, socioeconomic status, disabilities, available resources, community values, and support systems. This will require, of course, that you make the effort to get to know and understand these things.

Accommodating to the needs of your learners also means that you must engage in ongoing efforts to determine what your students already know and are able to do; you will have to analyze and evaluate their work with regularity to determine what it is you should teach next. The third-grade teacher who taught a lesson on subject-verb agreement because she had discovered that her students were having trouble with this skill was doing just that. But she was probably attentive to that competency in part because it is a State of California designated standard for the third-grade language arts curriculum. If so, this choice would be representative of the coming together of the two ends of the vertical axis, which asks you to consider such questions as: How does a student come to know this discipline? How might I teach this content to this group of learners? What is it that this particular student knows and does not know about this topic? Those who write about culturally relevant teaching (e.g., Ladson-Billings, 1994) can be helpful in this regard. According to Lee, Spencer, and Harpalani (2003),

> Cultural modeling calls on researchers and practitioners to examine the students' everyday practices, in their families and peer social networks, directing their attention toward processes of reasoning and habits of mind as well as toward naïve theories and misconceptions that may bear some relationship to a targeted set of specific concepts and strategies in a subject-matter discipline. (p. 8)

Lee et al. are explicitly addressing the need to draw on the strengths of particular students in helping them to learn specific subject matter knowledge. You can begin at either point, but both ends of the vertical axis and the interaction between them will need to be considered in deciding what to teach—the content of your lessons—and how to teach it—the pedagogical strategies you use. This is the horizontal axis: your planned curriculum and instruction. What actually happens, the implemented curriculum, is, as mentioned above, at the center.

The way in which I have described this heuristic tends to imply that you always begin with the vertical axis, either endpoint or both together, when you engage in principled planning. This is not necessarily the case. You can also begin with the horizontal axis. In actuality, you should always begin and end with the center, with reflections on your actual practice and its outcomes. But with that input to guide you, you might next identify new learning goals derived from student needs and interests in relationship to justifiable content standards and then select or design appropriate interventions. But you could also proceed to seek out possible curricular and pedagogical options, which you then select and modify according to your theories of teaching and learning. In the next section, we offer hypothetical and abbreviated examples of starting with the vertical axis and starting with the horizontal axis to engage in the principled planning of an elementary social studies lesson.

❖ PLANNING EXAMPLES

Vertical Axis Initiation

Catherine is a fifth-grade teacher who is in a reading group with other teachers of various grade levels at different schools; all of the teachers graduated from the same credential program and have remained friends. The latest readings they have been discussing are from a book called *Beyond Heroes and Holidays* (Lee, Menkart, & Okazawa-Rey, 1998). The James Banks (1998) chapter, wherein he describes four levels of multicultural curriculum reform, particularly impressed Catherine. She has always valued multicultural education and believes it to be a critical aspect of her social studies program. She feels that one of the central purposes of social studies education is to prepare students for the rights and responsibilities of world citizenship. To her, this includes understanding and appreciating different groups of people in the United States and around the world and their historical and current interdependence. What she realized, however, when applying Banks's framework to an analysis of her program, was that most of her lessons had been at the lower levels of his continuum: the Contributions Approach and the Ethnic Additive Approach. She decided that to better meet her newly articulated social studies goals, she had to design her lessons to be consistent with the higher levels: the Transformative Approach and the Decision-Making and Social Action Approach.

In this process, Catherine is working at the top of the vertical axis of our heuristic. With the help of both present (her teacher friends) and text-based (Banks) colleagues, she is reformulating and adding detail to her understanding of social studies. She has encountered a new perspective on the meaning and purpose of social studies education that is consistent with, but more focused and developed than her current view. Therefore, the new ideas are fairly easily incorporated into her existing conceptual framework. She understands, however, that before she can proceed to make the hoped-for changes in her curriculum and instruction, she will have to strengthen her knowledge of the subject matter. She teaches fifth grade in California, and the state framework specifies that the focus of her social studies program needs to be on American history, as is true of many other states. In order for her to design and implement units that are more consistent with the upper levels of Banks's (1998) continuum, she has to enhance her knowledge of that history from multiple perspectives. So she turns next to reading books such as Howard Zinn's (1997) *A People's History of the United States,* an endeavor that will continue for some time to come.

In the meantime, Catherine feels that she can begin to reconstruct her curriculum with these new aims and structures in mind. The next unit in her program is to be on the causes of the American Revolution, Standard 5.5 of the *History-Social Science Content Standards for California Public Schools* (California Department of Education, 2001). The details of that standard include the following:

1. Understand how political, religious, and economic ideas and interests brought about the Revolution (e.g., resistance to imperial policy, the Stamp Act, the Townshend Acts, taxes on tea, Coercive Acts)

2. Know the significance of the first and second Continental Congresses and of the Committees of Correspondence

3. Understand the people and events associated with the drafting and signing of the Declaration of Independence and the document's significance, including the key political concepts it embodies, the origins of those concepts, and its role in severing ties with Great Britain

4. Describe the views, lives, and impact of key individuals during this period (e.g., King George III, Patrick Henry, Thomas Jefferson, George Washington, Benjamin Franklin, John Adams) (pp. 2–3)

Catherine believes that these standards could still help to guide her new approach to the curriculum, but they would not be complete as stated. She has to embellish them by incorporating into Number 1, for instance, an understanding of the views of the British and the French.

For Numbers 2 through 4, she must include knowledge goals about the wives, families, and slaves who made it possible for these men to leave home for long periods of time and engage in this work. She will be sure her students come to understand the role that living among Native Americans played in the development of the colonists' views about society and government. She also wants her students to become familiar with the perspectives of those who were opposed to the Revolution. She consults resources that can help her to fill these gaps, including original newspaper accounts, diaries, and autobiographies and British and French textbooks on the war.

Before formulating her plans, Catherine needs to find out what her students already know or think they know about the causes of the Revolutionary War, as well as what they would like to know. In addition, she needs to understand how they are thinking about American history in general, both what it is and how it has been recorded and reported and why. She wants the children both to learn some history and to begin to think like historians. In focusing in this way on her students, Catherine is drawing on her knowledge of the bottom part of the vertical axis and its relationship to the top. She is inquiring into what her particular students might need and want to know about her identified subject matter goals. She is also drawing on her knowledge of learning theory to help her determine the best ways for them to come to know it. She believes for instance that learning will be enhanced if they can pursue their own questions, if they are actively engaged in investigation and problem solving, if they consult and critique a wide variety of primary documents, if they can both acquire and share information using their multiple intelligences, and if they interact and deliberate with one another and with her.

Catherine now draws on this information in attending to the horizontal axis of the heuristic: the planning of her curriculum and instruction. One sample lesson from her unit can illustrate what might result from this process. Toward the end of the unit, she includes a lesson in which the students work in groups to identify what strategies different constituencies employed to try to get their views known and thereby to influence the decision as to whether or not the colonies would engage in a war for independence. After brainstorming approaches taken, the students will analyze them according to which strategies were most and least successful and then engage in a discussion as to why that might be, which would include attention to who was employing the strategies and why. The lesson concludes with students making entries in their social studies journals, summarizing in words and drawings what they learned about efforts to influence public opinion during that period in American history. In a subsequent lesson, they will draw on those inferences to make decisions about how they might go about influencing a present-day political issue in their own communities, which they will eventually try to enact. One of the many reasons Catherine has for constructing this lesson is that it seems to embody her newly embraced goal of creating a multicultural curriculum that is consistent with Banks's (1998) fourth level, the Decision-Making and Social Action Approach.

As Catherine begins to implement the unit, she engages in constant monitoring of actual interactions and of the student work that results. She looks for developing understandings and areas of confusion and adjusts accordingly. She focuses her assessments on looking for evidence of what Banks (1998) describes as an understanding of "how the common U.S. culture and society emerged from a complex synthesis and interaction of the diverse cultural elements that originated within the various cultural, racial, ethnic, and religious groups that make up American society" (p. 75). She does not test for facts because that is not her goal; she looks to see whether or not students are learning to think like historians and are developing an understanding of the rights and responsibilities of citizenship, as evidenced in their written work, including their social studies journal, visual constructions, and oral presentations. If the students pose questions that she cannot answer, she tries to both enhance her own knowledge and direct them to resources that will help them find out for themselves. She reflects on her teaching by continuously asking herself questions like the following:

- What evidence do I have that the students are aware of and open to multiple perspectives on the events and issues leading to the Revolutionary War?
- What kinds of worthwhile historical questions are they asking and pursuing?
- Which students are not as engaged or making as much progress as the others, why might that be so, and what might I do about it?
- How are my pedagogies providing equal access to information for my three ELLs? How often do they share their views, and, when they do, are they analyzing and synthesizing information or just reciting facts?

Catherine explores these and other questions with feedback from her students and the support of her teacher colleagues. Her new unit (the horizontal axis), planned in accordance with her transformed theories about the nature and purpose of social studies education for her particular learners (the vertical axis), is a work in progress, a process not a product, a beginning not an end.

Horizontal Axis Initiation

Tyrone is a fourth-grade teacher in New York City. His school district has just adopted a new social studies curriculum, *Social Studies Alive!* (Bower & Lobdell, 2003). Tyrone is unsure about whether or not this new program will be consistent with his current views about social studies education for fourth graders in his context. He needs to determine to what extent and in what ways he might go about implementing this new program. First, he engages in a careful review of the fourth-grade curricular materials, beginning with the authors' stated intentions and rationales. In the introduction, Bower and Lobdell (2003) assert that their approach "consists of a series of instructional practices that allow students of all abilities to 'experience' history. These teaching methods were developed by teachers who carefully and thoughtfully combined . . . three educational theories" (p. vii). The three theories listed are Howard Gardner's theory of multiple intelligences, Elizabeth Cohen's theory of cooperative groupwork, and Jerome Bruner's idea of the spiral curriculum. The authors then proceed to explain how and why the student text is designed to enable and improve student reading comprehension. In this discussion, they emphasize the important role "anticipation" plays in the successful understanding of expository text. To support student development of this skill, they encourage the use of the KWL strategy, which includes the three-step process of having students recall what they *know*, determine what they *want* to know, and keep track of what they *learn* as they proceed.

Tyrone is encouraged by this information. He is not only familiar with but also in agreement with the three learning theories by which they claim to be guided. He will, of course, have to see for himself whether or not the curriculum is really consistent with these views when he examines and uses the actual lessons. Furthermore, KWL is a strategy already common in his pedagogy because it gives him important information about his students that can inform his teaching and gives them a voice in the determination of their own learning. He is also pleased that the authors have made an effort to make the text both accessible and instructive for the less-skilled readers in his class, again something he will have to test out for himself. The curriculum seems to be well grounded in learning theory, the bottom part of the vertical axis. Tyrone notices, however, that very little is said in the introduction about the authors' views on the discipline of social studies. He can find no explicit statement about their definition of social studies education or their overall aims for the program. Their position about the top portion of the vertical axis seems to be more implicit and will have to be inferred from the content and pedagogy of the individual and cumulative lessons.

Tyrone's next step, therefore, is to examine the texts and supporting materials. He first looks at the overall program and then scrutinizes a few sample lessons. This review is guided by his theories and values with regard to the teaching of social studies and his knowledge of the discipline, which he has found to be well represented by the position of the National Council for the Social Studies (NCSS) (1994). He also will check to see how well the curriculum addresses New York's relevant learning standards (New York State Education Department, 2003), which he considers to be generally appropriate.

What Tyrone finds is that the first lesson is framed by the question, What are the social sciences? The stated purpose is to help "students discover that the social sciences offer powerful ways to understand individuals and society" (Bower & Lobdell, 2003, p. iv). The social sciences included are economics, geography, political science, and history. The instructions to the teacher contain a suggestion:

> Explain to students that they will learn to become social scientists throughout the year and that this is the first lesson in their training as "junior social scientists." As the year progresses, they will put on different social scientist "hats" to develop different ways of thinking about human behavior. (p. 3)

This indicates to Tyrone that a clear goal of the program is to help the students learn to acquire the skills of social science and not just learn a series of disparate facts. This is consistent with NCSS's (1994) position, which not only emphasizes social studies as an integrated discipline but also aims to develop skills as well as knowledge. Likewise, it seems to be compatible with New York's learning standards for social studies, which use the same four disciplines to conceptualize the field. The authors also have a strong emphasis on the development of intellectual skills as opposed to itemized facts. A look at the whole table of contents in the teacher's guide suggests that the children will continue to learn about individuals and society through these different lenses over the course of the year, as well as consider how these various disciplinary perspectives might interrelate in efforts to understand and resolve human problems.

Also of critical importance to Tyrone is that there be equal representation of the voices and influences of the many racial and ethnic groups who have populated this land. Three of the four key ideas in New York's Standard 1 (New York State Education Department, 2003), which relates to the history of the United States and New York, emphasize this aspect:

- *Key Idea 1:* The study of New York State and United States history requires an analysis of the development of American culture, its diversity and multicultural context, and the ways people are unified by many values, practices, and traditions.
- *Key Idea 2:* Important ideas, social and cultural values, beliefs, and traditions from New York State and United States history illustrate the connections and interactions of people and events across time and from a variety of perspectives.
- *Key Idea 3:* Study about the major social, political, economic, cultural, and religious developments in New York State and United States history involves learning about the important roles and contributions of individuals and groups.

Tyrone detects many lessons (and lessons are multiday events in this program) that are either explicitly focused on the diversity issue— for example, Lesson 3 investigates The Peopling of the United States by multiple racial and ethnic groups—or inclusive of it—for example, an activity in Lesson 11 explores the question of Colorado River water use from the perspective of Native Americans, farmers, ranchers, Mexicans, and city dwellers.

Tyrone is getting the sense that this curriculum is in the main consistent with his theories of the teaching and learning of social studies. He does have two concerns about aspects that seem to be missing from the program. The first has to do with overall vision. NCSS (1994) stresses that the aim of social studies education is the promotion of civic competence: "The primary purpose of social studies is to help young people develop the ability to make informed and reasoned decisions for the public good as citizens of a culturally diverse, democratic society in an interdependent world" (p. 1). This curriculum does not seem to give explicit emphasis to this purpose. Bower and Lobdell (2003) talk about the importance of understanding human behavior but, at least in Tyrone's initial perusal of the program, not much about the ultimate aim of that understanding. This is something he will want to be sure to incorporate.

Tyrone's second concern also has to do with a missing piece. His fourth-grade social studies program has been focused on the State of New York. Bower and Lobdell (2003) take a regional rather than a state-focused approach. Tyrone assumes that this is because it is material designed for a national market. The last few chapters do provide a general structure for the students to investigate the geography, history, economy, and government of their state, which will be helpful in this regard, but he feels he will have to supplement this with some lessons from his previous curriculum. Because both of his concerns seem to entail supplementation rather than transformation, Tyrone feels positive about using this new curriculum. He recognizes, however, that he will need to give careful attention to each lesson as he proceeds and, if necessary, adapt it to fit his goals and the particular needs of his students.

To do so effectively, Tyrone, like Catherine, will have to engage in the ongoing monitoring of classroom interactions and student work. Because his whole school is implementing this new curriculum at the same time, Tyrone will arrange to work with the other fourth-grade teachers on this project. They will observe one another teach during their prep periods and solicit the help of parents to videotape lessons that the teachers can then watch and debrief together during grade-level meetings. With the help of his colleagues, Tyrone will reflect on his teaching of this content by repeatedly asking himself questions like the following:

- How is this individual lesson consistent with the learning theories of Gardner, Cohen, and Bruner?
- Is this lesson appropriate for my particular students, and, if not, what adaptations might I make? Are there any specific changes I need to create so that my two special-needs students can fully participate in and gain from this lesson?

- What connections am I making between lessons so that they will lead to enhanced social studies skills as well as greater knowledge of the history, government, economics, and geography of the State of New York in relationship to the rest of the country?
- How is the program helping my students "develop the ability to make informed and reasoned decisions for the public good as citizens of a culturally diverse, democratic society in an interdependent world" (NCSS, 1994, p. 1), and how can I tell?

In Tyrone's case, the curriculum and instruction—the horizontal axis—has already been constructed by others; his job will be to adapt, adjust, supplement, and replace that program according to both his pre-existing theories of the teaching and learning of social studies and what he discovers from his ongoing reflection on what actually happens during and as a result of implementation. This process may alter his original theories and values, the vertical axis.

❖ THE PRINCIPLED PLANNING AND IMPLEMENTATION OF SUBJECT MATTER IN AN ERA OF REGULATION AND HIGH-STAKES TESTING

The cases of Tyrone and Catherine are hypothetical and brief. You are not meant to conceive of them as ideals or even models—certainly not as recipes to follow. They are instead intended to provide you with images of the possible with regard to the principled planning and implementation of lessons and units that will contribute to the development of powerful subject matter knowledge for all of your students. They present scenarios that illustrate some of the complexity of practice and the importance of context-sensitive decision making. The cases emphasize the notion that curricular planning and instruction needs to be an ongoing, collegial process of reflective deliberation about your teaching and your students' learning, informed by well-justified, ever-developing conceptualizations of the disciplines, theories of teaching and learning, and moral, ethical, and political values and aims. The cases demonstrate that the heuristic can be used flexibly and responsively to help you both create and design your own curriculum and evaluate and adapt existing lessons and units appropriately. It is an approach that is consistent with the positive aspects of the current climate of standards-based reform and resistant to the more negative qualities.

The nobler motivation behind standards-based reform is the desire to have all students develop substantive disciplinary knowledge, an equity agenda with which we certainly agree. The question is not whether we should have standards but which standards and decided by whom. In addition, as a recent study by the American Federation of Teachers (AFT) (2001) would suggest, we need to problematize how those standards might be achieved and assessed. Strong advocates of what they refer to as coherent standards-based *systems,* the AFT decided to investigate how well the country was doing with regard to this effort. In their view, standards-based reform is an ordered process that includes "well-developed standards and a curriculum to support their implementation; professional development for teachers; new assessments aligned to the standards; and fair incentives and sufficient resources to help students make the grade" (p. 9). What the AFT found is that all states have set or are setting common academic standards for students and that the quality of those standards is improving, according to their criteria (p. 25). While encouraging in general, the findings lend credence to our suggestion that you cannot simply accept at face value the particular standards in your state. They can be one of many possible guides for your standard-setting endeavors.

Far more problematic are the other aspects of the reform system. The AFT (2001) discovered that curriculum construction with accompanying professional development had only just begun. Thus, programs and resources for the implementation of standards-based instruction, the necessary next step, had yet to be achieved. Nonetheless, many states were skipping right to the assessment of those nonexistent programs. This inherently flawed approach has resulted in the following:

- Many state assessment programs are based on weak standards.
- Many state assessment programs use tests unaligned to their standards.
- A number of states use results from nonaligned tests to hold back students or deny them a diploma.
- Many states impose sanctions on students but fail to mandate intervention and to provide the resources to help them. (p. 34)

Further exacerbating the problem, according to James Popham (2001), is the use of high-stakes standardized achievement tests that not only are *not* aligned with particular state standards but also are absolutely incapable of doing what standards-based reform assessments need to do—"ascertain the caliber of students' schooling" (p. 74). The impact of this misguided approach to educational reform is most catastrophic for the very students it was originally intended to benefit. The previously underserved students are the ones most often sanctioned, held back, and denied diplomas (AFT, 2001; Popham, 2001) under the current systems. In addition, the overall effect has been "curricular reductionism," focused on low-level cognitive skills and a preponderance of "drill and kill" test preparation exercises (Popham, 2001) that again diminish the long-term opportunities for those same students. In fear of threatened retributions, schools are trading marginal short-term gains on inappropriate measures for the deep understanding of subject matter necessary for subsequent high-level work and educational progress.

But as Popham (2001) also argues, we cannot absolve ourselves of responsibility for these difficulties. We have not fully embraced our professional responsibilities with regard to curriculum and its assessment. As a result, others are trying to do so for us and in ill-informed and often harmful ways. We urge you, therefore, to act as professionals by taking a principled approach to the planning, implementation, and evaluation of subject matter instruction. You need to continue to build your understanding and expertise with regard to both the vertical axis of the heuristic—knowledge of the discipline, knowledge of learners and learning, and the relationship between the two—and the horizontal—awareness and understanding of multiple, viable teaching strategies and existing or potential curricula. You need to continuously reflect on your implemented curriculum and its outcomes with the help of your students, colleagues, and the educational literature, asking always about who is benefiting and to what ends. In some schools and districts that have overly prescribed and narrowly focused curricula or high-stakes and misaligned testing, due to a lack of faith in your professional expertise, this will be a greater, but all the more pressing challenge. Even in such circumstances, a principled approach should help you to incorporate seemingly small adjustments that can make a big difference in contributing to your efforts to enable all of your students to progress in developing in-depth subject matter knowledge that will have long-term as well as short-term benefits. Especially important is to help your students engage in sustained, well-justified learning experiences, where connections between and among activities, ideas, concepts, and skills are constructed. You have the professional and moral responsibility to ensure that your curriculum will not be "just a series of fun, or even not-so-fun activities" that lead your learners nowhere in particular.

❖ REFERENCES

American Federation of Teachers. (2001). *Making standards matter 2001.* Washington, DC: Author.

Ball, D. L., & Bass, H. (2000). Interweaving content and pedagogy in teaching and learning to teach: Knowing and using mathematics. In J. Boaler (Ed.), *Multiple perspectives on the teaching and learning of mathematics* (pp. 83–104). Westport, CT: Ablex.

Banks, J. A. (1998). Approaches to multicultural curriculum reform. In E. Lee, D. Menkart, & M. Okazawa-Rey (Eds.), *Beyond heroes and holidays: A practical guide to K-12 anti-racist, multicultural education and staff development* (pp. 74–75). Washington, DC: Network of Educators on the Americas.

Bower, B., & Lobdell, J. (2003). *Social studies alive!* Palo Alto, CA: Teachers' Curriculum Institute.

California Department of Education. (November 2001) *History-social science content standards for California public schools.* Retrieved August 12, 2003, from http://www.cde.ca.gov/standards/history/grade5.html

Driver, R., Asoko, H., Leach, J., Mortimer, E., & Scott, P. (1994). Constructing scientific knowledge in the classroom. *Educational Researcher, 23*(7), 5–12.

Freeman, Y. S., & Freeman, D. E. (2002). *Closing the achievement gap: How to reach limited-formal-schooling and long-term English learners.* Portsmouth, NH: Heinemann.

Gardner, H. (1991). *The unschooled mind: How children think and how schools should teach them.* New York: Basic Books.

Haberman, M. (2000). Urban schools: Day camps or custodial centers? *Phi Delta Kappan, 82*(3), 203–208.

Kovalik, S. (1997). *Integrated thematic instruction: The model* (3rd ed.). Kent, WA: Discovery Press.

Kumashiro, K. K. (2001). "Posts" perspectives on anti-oppressive education in social studies, English, mathematics, and science classrooms. *Educational Researcher, 30*(3), 3–12.

Ladson-Billings, G. (1994). *The dreamkeepers: Successful teachers of African American children.* San Francisco: Jossey-Bass.

Lee, C. D., Spencer, M. B., & Harpalani, V. (2003). "Every shut eye ain't sleep": Studying how people live culturally. *Educational Researcher, 32*(5), 6–13.

Lee, E., Menkart, D., & Okazawa-Rey, M. (1998). *Beyond heroes and holidays: A practical guide to K-12 anti-racist, multicultural education and staff development.* Washington, DC: Network of Educators on the Americas.

Lewis, N., & Johnson, J. (2002). Finding post-modernity in elementary classrooms. In C. Kosnik, A. Freese, & A. P. Samaras (Eds.), *Making a difference in teacher education through self-study: Proceedings of the fourth international conference on self-study of teacher education practices, Herstmonceux, East Sussex, England* (Vol. 2, pp. 57–61). Toronto, ON: University of Toronto, OISE.

National Council for the Social Studies (NCSS). (1994). *Expectations of excellence: Curriculum standards for social studies.* Washington DC: NCSS Publications.

New York State Education Department. (2003). *New York state learning standards.* Retrieved August 13, 2003 from http://www.emsc.nysed.gov/ciai/socst/ssls.html

Peregoy, S. F., & Boyle, O. F. (2001). *Reading, writing, and learning in ESL.* New York: Longman.

Popham, W. J. (2001). *The truth about testing: An educator's call to action.* Alexandria, VA: Association for Supervision and Curriculum Development.

Schoenfeld, A. H. (2002). Making mathematics work for all children: Issues of standards, testing, and equity. *Educational Researcher, 31*(1), 13–25.

Schwab, J. J. (1964). The structure of the disciplines: Meanings and significances. In G. W. Ford & L. Pugno (Eds.), *The structure of knowledge and the curriculum* (pp. 6–30). Chicago: Rand McNally.

Wilson, S. M. (2001). Research on history teaching. In V. Richardson (Ed.), *Handbook of research on teaching* (4th ed., pp. 27–544). New York: Macmillan.

Wilson, S. M. (2003). *California dreaming: Reforming mathematics education.* New Haven, CT: Yale University Press.

Zinn, H. (1997). *A people's history of the United States.* New York: New Press.

6

Teaching to Collaborate, Collaborating to Teach

Ruth Cossey

Philip Tucher

❖　❖　❖

An hour before the starting bell at Edgewater High, student teachers Colleen and Tessa arrived to set up for the day's buoyancy lesson. They wanted to provide students with easy access to both highly technical and everyday ordinary equipment needed for the six planned experiments. Near the front entrance, for example, hanging over the edge of a huge vat of water was a piece of rope attached to a bag of more than a thousand pennies resting below the water's surface. A wall chart guided the physics students through the activity they were to complete, even before class officially began.

AUTHORS' NOTE: All the names used in this chapter are pseudonyms.

With a partner lift this bag both under water and outside the water. Write your names and your estimate of the weight in both cases. Comment on any observations you have about this phenomenon.

Colleen surveyed the classroom; she thought her students would find it inviting although maybe a bit intimidating. Tessa, who had volunteered to be the teaching assistant for the day, quickly sighted all the materials on her checklist while Colleen silently rehearsed the sequence of instruction she and the other nine teacher candidates had planned. All was ready. Colleen only hoped that her students, accustomed to a few visitors at a time, wouldn't be overwhelmed by the presence of not only her cooperating teacher, Mr. Zales, but also the videographer, several college professors, and the host of mathematics and science teacher candidates. While she taught the class, her colleagues would collect data related to the agreed-upon research theme.

Students would come to appreciate the importance of struggle and respect for others' ideas as integral to the learning process.

———————

At 3:30 that afternoon the teacher candidates held a formal research-lesson-debriefing meeting. Each of them had taken about an hour to analyze—if tentatively—the particular data they gathered during class. A few more college professors joined the audience along with the school's vice principal. Colleen summarized her reactions to that morning's class: a critical incident along the path of a 2-month research lesson cycle. Near the end of her 10-minute remarks, she added

. . . In general the theme for doing this is time. It's such a time-intensive process. I know that any time you do things as a group, it takes as much time as it would have if you multiply ordinary time by the number of people in the group. That's just how long it takes. And it's often a much better product, and you learn a huge amount doing it, but I have my daughter saying things to me like "Can I go to Shauna's house 'cause I get attention there and I don't at home." And things like, "How come we only get to work on your projects?" . . . It's been fun. I really, I liked doing it. I didn't have time to do it, but I really enjoyed the process.

Teaching is hard—too hard to attempt in isolation. The promise of collegiality is far too great to ignore. Yet, Colleen's statement about time illustrates one of the many tensions teachers and learners of all ages and contexts struggle with as we strive to reap the benefits of collaboration. This chapter springs from the core belief that learning occurs in relationships. Clearly, the education of both students of teachers and students of teaching can be greatly enhanced by interaction. The work of teaching and learning to teach requires attention to several important principles. As explored in other chapters, we will need to make sense of the political implications of our work and attend to the developmental needs of our students within an ethic of care while reflecting and deciding on the most appropriate content of a lesson or unit of study. The magnitude of the work of learning to teach cannot be overstated. You do not have to—and perhaps you cannot—put all of this together alone. The rest of this chapter will ask you to also consider pursuing a principled practice of collegiality as integral to your professional development. You will examine several facets of collaboration, including dilemmas resolved within the context of collaborating to teach and teaching to collaborate. Throughout the chapter, you will find a lack of precision in the use of the words *collegiality, collaboration, cooperation,* and their derivatives. Simply put, the words will refer to folks talking, thinking, and working together and not to any particular set of practices.

❖ GETTING SMARTER TOGETHER: COMMUNITIES OF PRACTICE

In Chapter 4, you read about constructivism as a theory of learning. Ask any Piagetian or Vygotskian; he or she will tell you that social interaction is critical to individual knowledge development. Here, we would like you to consider that individuals are not the only ones who get smarter as a result of good interactions; communities can also gain knowledge and become able to do and think things that the individuals of the community would find hard or impossible to achieve alone. In social interaction, individuals co-construct knowledge by negotiating new meanings through their engagement in mutual activities. Even on those occasions when we believe we do our learning in isolation, we generally rely on the previous work of others; for example, writing and auditory or visual images. Furthermore, even when aspects of our work are done in solitude, we typically make sense of required tasks in the context of having to prepare for, or receive feedback from, an audience other than ourselves. Hence, much of what is considered to be solitary knowledge contributions can be traced to intentional or unintentional group efforts.

Of course, not every group exchange fosters learning or facilitates new knowledge and growth. Wenger (1998) reminds us that communities can reinforce shared and erroneous stereotypes or produce "tried-and- failed" solutions to problems. Fullan (1993) also cautions that we must learn to differentiate between group collaboration and "group-think" because, in groups, individual creativity, difference, and even responsibility can become stymied or silenced. In groups, a lack of focus or common purpose can result in a scattering of efforts and, at best, a waste of time. Despite widespread agreement that human beings have a predisposition towards co-constructing meaning, there is abundant evidence that school classrooms and teacher lounges are not automatically settings for nondysfunctional learning communities. Collegiality, taken as a principle of practice, however, can help you harness the power of community to expand exponentially your professional efforts to teach and learn.

❖ LEARNING TO COLLABORATE: HAVING PRODUCTIVE INTERACTIONS

Successful collaborations depend on seemingly contradictory premises. There needs to be diversity among the collaborators, but participants must share a number of cultural practices. The diversity will allow the group to probe teaching and learning issues through a richness of multiple perspectives. It is especially through difference—in perception, in areas of expertise, and in experience both in and outside the classroom—that the group will avoid simply reinforcing the status quo. On the other hand, interpersonal communication requires that the group either initially or eventually come to share some common language, common goals, and, to some extent, an agreed-on range of acceptable patterns of work and interaction.

Wenger (1998) considers two components of community theory: *participation* and *reification*. The first of these, participation, relates to being a "part of things." Lave and Wenger (1991) and Rogoff (1995) suggest that an individual's participation in a group activity can range from peripheral to very active. Participation is intricately linked to individual identity formation relative to the group. Wenger, Lave, and Rogoff posit that an individual's identity can radically affect her or his individual knowledge development and contribution to the group. Who you are in the group is affected by your own previous experience and understanding, your own role in the group knowledge construction, and what you ultimately take away from the experience in the group (Cohen & Lotan, 1995).

Reification refers to taking the experiences of the group interactions and transforming them into artifacts or words that can be interpreted by group members and others as new knowledge. This new knowledge, fruit of the group's labor, can remind individuals within the group of the shared values and vision toward which the group is moving. Thus, in the classroom, as students reflect on their learning process during a particular activity, a teacher might "coin" a way of remembering a lesson learned: helping doesn't mean giving answers; no one of us is as smart as all of us together; there are many ways to skin a cat!—to name a few. To assist students in internalizing new and common expectations of the group, teachers can help "lessons learned" become integral to classroom practice as they are referenced repeatedly while the community develops.

What would these ideas of participation and reification mean for you as you look for and work toward meaningful collaboration with other adults? In the most effective communities, people agree that difference is an important asset of the group. If group members appreciate diversity and actively strive to see and use the different strengths of others and of themselves, generally more and better work will get done and status issues will be markedly less disruptive. Working with people who know how to—or are really interested in learning how to—work across differences results in more productive activity, but such cooperative productive activity is not that simply accomplished. Minimally, such collaboration requires community members to have highly developed listening skills and to exhibit a willingness to be flexible, possibly beyond each person's initial area of comfort. Good collaborations are almost always safe, but they are typically at some point uncomfortable. Let us turn to the examination of one collaborative structure you may find available to you to consider further some of the determinants of fruitful collaboration.

❖ COLLABORATIVE PLANNING
   FOR INSTRUCTION: LESSON STUDY

You will remember Colleen and her colleagues. They were engaged in collective lesson conceptualization and implementation in a process of professional development borrowed originally from Japan in the form of lesson study (Lewis, 2002). Variations of this practice are becoming common in the United States and are often the nexus of school/ university and other institutional partnerships.

Why would the group of preservice math and science teachers want to engage in collaboration such as lesson study? What knowledge about learning and teaching did they seek to gain? Colleen was teaching a course in physics open to all students in her public high school. She knew that in two months she would be faced with the problem of having her students master buoyancy beyond what they had intuited in elementary and middle school. She wanted to get them to a precollege-level understanding of the forces involved in floating or sinking objects as an instantiation of general knowledge about forces working on the world. This was her first year teaching high school students, and she did not know their general knowledge level. Given her own uncertainty about what would be expected of her and her students in a general physics class, Colleen eagerly volunteered when her group of novice teachers had to choose a member around whose class they would design and teach a research lesson.

What was in it for Colleen's colleagues? Lesson study, a two-month focus of their curriculum and instruction class, would provide hands-on experiences of an inquiry approach to thorough lesson planning and revision. Through the lesson study inquiry cycle, this cohort of teachers would have opportunities to clarify and define their individual visions, goals, and objectives for students. By building on shared experiences with a particular research lesson and diverse interpretations of classroom events—both predicted and actual—the lesson study process also would provide rich opportunities for understanding and talking about students and learning. Success of the collaboration not only would deepen, but ultimately depend on the novice teachers' recognition and appreciation of each other's independent expertise.

Let's take a look at specific activities Colleen and her colleagues undertook. Their work revolved around three highly connected phases of instruction: goal setting and planning for instruction, teaching and observing students, and reflection and analysis of learning. Through lesson study, the group of teachers cycled through several iterations of this planning, teaching, and reflecting process.

❖ PLANNING TO TEACH COLLEEN'S STUDENTS

First, the group of teachers looked hard at their own students to identify a general set of long-term goals for instruction. What attributes of their students as learners—and, in this case, as powerful knowers of science and math—would they focus on together? What would be the theme of their inquiry? These teachers attended to notions of *intellective competence* to help them look even further than their strong desire to have students meet challenging content goals. According to Gordon (1999), the "intellective competence" needed by all citizens in the next century is truly demanding. They will be expected

> to bring rational order to chaos, bring knowledge and technique to the solution of problems, to test ideas against explicit and implicit moral values as well as against data, to think critically, and to recognize the relationship between concrete and abstract data.

Intellective competence must orchestrate affective, cognitive, and "situative contexts" directed at purposeful ends. In short, "these academic achievements are less focused on what children know and do and more sharply focused on what we want learners to become—compassionate and thinking members of a community" (p. 1).

The group then cemented the curricular foci of their work by selecting a specific class of students: Colleen's third-period physics class at Edgewater High. With a tentative research theme and a central content topic in mind, the group began planning a lesson that would eventually be taught and revised twice before being taught again as part of an on-site visit to one teacher's school and classroom.

In a healthy collaboration, participants, whether in peripheral or leading positions, have roles and responsibilities and are comfortable in knowing that they are welcome to become as involved as they desire. Every member of the team finds active ways to help create and shape the task. During the lesson study process, some participants researched existing lessons on the topic; some surveyed the literature and experienced teachers for information about common misconceptions high school youngsters held about forces in general and buoyancy in particular; and some drafted the preliminary plan. To clarify their research theme and predictions of possible student responses to the lesson, different volunteers, in pairs, taught the lesson twice to one another. During this peer teaching, each participant's role was clear. The pair doing the teaching made detailed pedagogical decisions. The other teachers, then in the role of high school students, focused on analyzing and predicting students' responses for each part of the lesson. In this way, each teacher provided an individual perspective and critique on how the lesson would challenge and engage students, thus bringing to life the research theme(s) driving the whole endeavor.

Through the collaborative process of lesson study, this group of teachers prepared a lesson both to support students learning physics and to develop in students an intellective competency. As a result of this lesson, the teachers hypothesized, students would apply reasoning about Newton's Laws to fluids and also discover and apply Archimedes' Law through guided experimentation and problem solving. Moreover, students would further develop an appreciation for the importance of struggle with challenges and respect for others' ideas as integral to the learning process. The learning goals of this lesson were both academic and social. Students (as well as teachers) would learn to value and productively make use of processes of collaboration. Thus, collegiality was a learning goal as well as a process to learn.

Planning to Learn From Colleen's Students

Not only did Colleen and her colleagues plan the physics lesson, they also collaborated on the research they would conduct during the class period to help them evaluate the effectiveness of their instructional plan. What would they each do as the students in the room were engaged in learning about buoyancy, and supposedly struggling and respecting one another's ideas, as part of the learning process? We could ask more generally: When teachers are observing a lesson in a colleague's classroom, what can they do to further a shared collaborative endeavor? In this case, in preparation for the research lesson, each of Colleen's colleagues defined a focus question that fit under the umbrella of the research theme. Each teacher arrived at the research lesson ready to document students' involvement in the lesson.

Considering the research theme related to struggle, for example, one teacher looked at issues of gender: Would male and female students show signs of struggle in different ways? Would patterns emerge suggesting that gender impacts the ways in which peers show respect for their classmates' ideas? Another teacher became interested in the detailed learning contexts in which struggle occurs: Did struggle during whole-class discussion differ from struggle during small-group lab time? One teacher wanted to study student questions—any and all of the questions uttered by students during the lesson. She developed a kind of taxonomy of question asking to categorize the varied questions she heard. Would question asking substantiate struggle? Would struggle lead to question asking? Taking a different approach, one teacher wanted to develop a narrative about one student's experience with the lesson. He followed a single student for the whole 90 minutes—a student still learning English, in this case—and documented as best he could her interactions with the materials, the language, her classmates, and so on. Through careful observation and recording, this teacher was able to convey a detailed account of struggle, but through the eyes of a single student.

As these examples suggest, individual teachers were responsible for defining and highlighting one facet of the shared research themes. Individual abilities to articulate a focus question and hypothesis, design an instrument for data collection, and study the student interactions during the lesson combined to provide richly overlapping data: stories, clumped lists, tallies, and utterances. Shared though the research theme was, each teacher found individual significance in the details of how the lesson had been crafted.

The back and forth between the shared learning of the group and the individual growth for participants is critical to the value of shared work. In developing consensus and crafting research themes, the group was moving toward a shared vision of students' learning. Each individual came to the group's consensus by a different path. In defining goals and a plan for a single shared lesson, individual teachers held different specific priorities within that plan. Even as the lesson was enacted, first among peers and then with high school students, individuals pursued different specific lines of exploration within the shared research theme. Each part of the collaboration included movement toward a shared purpose, with support coming from—and for—the specific contributions and talents of the individuals. This dynamic interaction between common action and individual growth gives generative purpose to collegial effort.

The Teaching Day

The day of the site visit involved so much more than the 90-minute physics class. After a brief orientation meeting, with school map and a schedule for the day in hand, the group dispersed to observe a variety of classroom lessons for the first hour and a half to get the flavor of a typical Tuesday in math or science class. A panel of students representing a cross-section of students at the school gave their perspectives on life as math or science students. Edgewater High teachers joined in discussions about current areas of interest for their school and departments. Then, just before the start of third period, it was off to Colleen's room. The team had decided on the following directions for themselves: Be there on time. Find your agreed-on observation post and have your observation materials ready. Introduce yourself to students as appropriate, but then be as unobtrusive as possible—yes, along with the videographer, the few college faculty members, and the cooperating teacher, as unobtrusive as possible.

After the research lesson was completed and the flurry of observation subsided, to celebrate and appreciate the students' hard work, the novice teachers and physics students sat down to enjoy pizza. The luncheon provided an opportunity for the teacher cohort to listen to the students as they reflected on the lesson and talked about their current and past experiences learning math and science.

For many teachers in the group, the most intense work began later that afternoon. That's when the tough questions started. What had they observed? Were their hypotheses about how this lesson would impact student interaction and learning confirmed, or did surprises rule the day? Did they have enough evidence to make a case? What if their data collection tools were hopelessly unrealistic? What if they didn't like the lesson?

With about an hour to process their whole morning, teachers worked in the relative quiet of the now-vacant cafeteria to prepare their comments for the research lesson debrief meeting. In pairs, they would tell their stories to the whole group. They would share their question, their data, and their findings. Together, the group would try to address their agreed-on research themes. What had they learned? What did they now know about the ways in which teachers come to know subject matter better for themselves as well as responding to the need to increase students' knowledge of physics? What did they now know about bringing to life a vision for active involvement in learning: the role of struggle and respect for others' ideas in the learning process?

Reflecting on the Lesson Study Experience

Through lesson study, teachers in the cohort had many formal and informal opportunities to reflect on the lesson taught and the lessons learned by students and teachers alike. This group of teachers developed a newer, broader set of issues and questions to think about when considering their students and their own practice. They reported knowing better how to observe their students for evidence of understanding. They had a better appreciation for the rigors of collecting data about their own teaching practices. They were able to use the lesson study process to further examine their instruction of students who were developing English language skills in addition to learning mathematics and science content. Some of the teachers indicated that they were becoming better judges of general cognitive workload placed on individuals during a lesson. Colleen noted, for example, that in some instances it was clear the teacher did more work, more thinking and reasoning preparing the lesson, than any of the students were required to do to enact the lesson. In those cases, she hypothesized that the notion of struggle was undermined by teacher simplification of student work.

A common tension emerged for the group about the role of confusion in learning for their students. Under some circumstances, and with some content, it is best to refine a lesson with the intent of removing all ambiguity for the students. On the other hand, there are times when it is critically important to refine lessons with the intent of injecting enough ambiguity to encourage students to think and reason with the mathematical and scientific concepts. Teachers need to provide students with sufficient opportunity to engage with a balance of exercise, conceptual development, and problem solving. However, when, under what circumstances, for which students, and with what material?—these questions gave life to the investigation. These are the considerations that made the inquiry worthy of the collaborative effort.

❖ DETERMINANTS OF A FRUITFUL COLLABORATION

As we look back on the lesson study experiences of Colleen and her colleagues, what are the implications for the rest of us? What are the overriding benefits of their collaboration beyond the particulars of lesson study? The promise of a principled, collegial practice is that in talking, thinking, and working together we become both individually and collectively wiser about the needs of our students, more aware of the importance of our colleagues' perspectives, and more efficacious in the shared work of teaching.

What will make a collaborative effort worth your while? What are the parameters and constraints that you might consider when thinking about collaboration? First, you might ask yourself if the project you and your colleagues are considering is sufficiently complex and interesting to each of you so that the time you spend working together will lead to greater understanding in areas that matter most to you and your students. There is no use teaming up when one person believes there is only one reasonable way to get the job done. Nor is there a need for collaboration when one person alone could complete the project more effectively. Instead, tasks that are inherently complex are more likely to be worthy of collaborative effort. When there is not an obvious answer or resolution to a problem, multiple perspectives and contributions yield a more successful outcome, and the group grows together in their individual and collective understanding of the situation and of each other. Know that you are likely to get more out of a collaborative effort if you are working on a topic that is truly of importance and interest to you. (Though, at times, heightened interest is the result of close study, and you may only realize halfway into a problem where the interest will come for you. Still, when it comes to decision time about whether a particular task is suitable for collaboration, a "don't-sweat-the-small-stuff" approach can be a useful rule of thumb.)

Second, consider asking whether each individual has something in particular to examine through the collaboration. An individual focus—and sometimes even an individual motivation—combines with a shared group focus to further and deepen the inquiry for both individuals and the group. These individual foci may be agreed on as interesting by the group as a whole, or they may be of interest, initially, only to some of you. But eventually, what you investigate individually will contribute to a more complicated and deeper understanding of the issue. If the task is worth this shared effort, this should be your goal.

Third, in your collaboration, do you hold a diversity of perspectives? If you do, you are likely as a group to learn a great deal more about the issue than if you all agree from the beginning. As we noted earlier, this diversity of perspectives leads to a richer understanding but also requires focused practice of active listening and respect for differing points of view.

Last, you know that any collaborative enterprise will take time, and time is one of the most precious commodities you have as a professional. Collaboration is time intensive. You will have to ask—just as Colleen did toward the end of the research lesson debriefing meeting—whether a collaborative effort is worth your time. While the trade-off between *time spent* and *learning gained* is not always evident from the beginning of a project, being able to stand back and assess how a project is going is an important ongoing aspect of working collaboratively. You, and those with whom you collaborate, can practice this stepping-back process of introspection and reflection.

While these four aspects of collaborative work are important, they are but the nuts and bolts of working together. Yes, collaboration takes place best when the task at hand is both compelling and complex for the participants in the group. Yes, it is important for individuals to identify their own particular areas of interest within a shared endeavor. It is true that groups do well when they pay close attention and ensure that diverse contributions and perspectives become heard and valued. When groups cultivate a self-reflective awareness, they are better able to adjust and adapt to the many pressures, including time, that surface along the way. Yet, these aspects of fruitful collaboration are important to the group's learning—and ultimately the learning of individual participants—because the learning and the subsequent learning of the students takes place in relationships.

❖ COLLABORATION IS ABOUT RELATIONSHIPS

The substance of collaborative work is contained in the nature of the relationships that teachers develop. At issue are relationships with content ideas as well as relationships with students. For example, teachers consider curriculum and pedagogy in terms of district, state, and national mandates but also in light of the general strengths and learning needs of their students. However, this task of choosing carefully sequenced, rich lessons is rife with pitfalls and booby traps. Multiple paths are important for content delivery to students who think differently than each other and you; therefore, we benefit from access to teachers who can help us think about the content and pedagogy differently also.

Our goal is to be powerful teachers and to empower all our students in their learning. No one teacher's view is going to be multifaceted enough to make sense of 20 students' understandings nor to anticipate the learning needs of 20 diverse students. Collaboration in forming lessons helps to reveal the nuances of the concepts, to hone the important points, and to generate ways to imagine how students might encounter the core ideas. As you are learning to teach, it is especially useful to have others' ideas to point out directions that students' thinking might go. A good curriculum is never enough, however. Curricular soundness is both enhanced and limited by the quality of the relationships among the human beings in the classroom.

Building relationships with and between students can be aided by professional conversations across race, ethnic, religious, and class boundaries. It is not that one teacher's white Judaic background, for example, will mean that he or she has necessarily more insight than a Christian African-American teacher into what lessons would be more accessible to white Jewish students in any given class. But it is evident that the educational establishment in this country is organized to present the first teacher with experiences that are more similar to those of the white Jewish students than are the world experiences of the second teacher. When these teachers work together, they both have the benefit of each other's distinct worldviews. Together, they also can reinforce for each other their common belief that knowing something about a specific cultural practice tells nothing for sure about any individual, but that knowledge about specific cultural practices can produce a higher level of questions to wonder about students' understanding.

Teaching is a profession rooted in optimism. Teachers are in very real ways keepers of the hope of the nation. We are privileged to behold on a daily basis the promise of sustained democracy through our interactions with students of all stages of civic maturity. Still, not every minute of each day sings with fulfillment. Sometimes, the sheer volume of work, or the inconsistency of the voices of those outside the profession who would try to define our job for us, overwhelms us. Teaching is a profession where the burnout rate is unacceptably high.

So we return to the power of relationships. Consider the nurturing effect that collegial interactions would have for you if you were a teacher new to a school: the sense of calm strength you feel when your new colleagues include and welcome you into the learning community; the sense of belonging and relief you feel when you see that the group will take a "divide and conquer" approach to many of the mundane tasks that you know will need to get done; and the sense of integrity and purpose you feel as the group begins to define shared areas of inquiry, because each person in this learning community is finding new insights into their work.

Because you were not looking for easy answers or simple recipes, and you did not expect to make sense of this most difficult work alone, your persistence can be born out of accountability to and support from collegial arrangements. Indeed, our colleagues can help sustain us; our collegial relationships can keep us hopeful; and our professional friends can keep us solidly heading in directions aligned with our moral compass. We hold the hope, the vision of a nation transformed by a well-educated enlightened populace. We can hold this vision and contribute to its enactment, in part because we move in professional communities that provide sounding boards, safety, and trust.

❖ CONCLUDING THOUGHTS

Nearly every "how to teach" text will include the importance of working together with other adults to meet the needs of your students. You will be asked to partner with many colleagues in a variety of contexts: with teachers who teach the same course or grade level, with teachers who share the same group of students, and with colleagues and administrators concerned about the same student-discipline issue. You will have opportunities to work side by side with parents, one of you desperate, perhaps, to see progress from a child still struggling to find her or his way in school. You will collaborate, too, with administrators, who must also evaluate your performance; and you will work with colleagues who are serving as union leaders, dedicated to the profession and to your employee rights and opportunities. Thus, you will be asked to collaborate in many settings so that, with support from this group of colleagues, you might teach your students well.

No less important, you will also have to explore what it means to teach others—your students—to engage meaningfully in collaborative work. As you learn to articulate your own priorities for collaboration, you can ask yourself how to support your students to make sense for themselves out of the same collaborative interactions and dynamics. As you think about your students becoming powerful thinkers and doers, where do you and they most need to focus? How will you learn more about your students? How will you decide on appropriate tasks to select? Are the tasks you select sufficiently complex and compelling to merit their collaborative effort? When will you coach them directly? When will you structure their learning so that they work together without your direct involvement? How will you ensure they get a productive balance of individual and collaborative assignments? As students learn to collaborate, their ability to participate fully in a democracy will develop. Because our goals for them are not only about academic achievement, the development of this civic and civil understanding is a good thing.

A principled approach to collegial practice suggests that careful thought about human relationships can shape the ways in which you are able to come to know your students and their learning. Collaboration is not just a principle for your practice as you think about your adult colleagues. Rather, it is a source of knowledge for both you and your students. Understanding that learning is a process of co-construction, accomplished more fully in collegial, respectful, diverse contexts, you place yourself alongside those with whom you partner, ready to support our young people to participate in a democratic society that promotes the success of all its citizens.

❖ REFERENCES AND SUGGESTED READINGS

Brown, J. S., Collins, A., & Duguid, P. (1989). Situated cognition and the culture of learning. *Educational Researcher, 18*, 32–42.

Cohen, E. G., & Lotan, R. A. (1995). Producing equal status interaction in the heterogeneous classroom. *American Educational Research Journal, 32*, 99–120.

Cole, M., & Engestrom, Y. (1993). A cultural historic approach to distributed cognition. In G. Salomon (Ed.), *Distributed cognitions* (pp. 1–46). Cambridge, UK: Cambridge University Press.

Dewey, J. (1997). *Democracy and education: An introduction to the philosophy of education.* Simon & Schuster. (Original work published 1916)

Fullan, M. (1993). *Change forces: Probing the depths of educational reform.* New York: Falmer.

Gordon, E. (1999). *Minority student achievement network conference report.* Retrieved from http://www.eths.k12.il.us.

Lave, J., & Wenger, E. (1991). *Situated learning: Legitimate peripheral participation.* New York: Cambridge University Press.

Lewis, C. C. (2002). *Lesson study: A handbook of teacher-led instructional change.* Philadelphia: Research for Better Schools.

Lewis, C., & Tschuchida, I. (1998, Winter). A lesson is like a swiftly flowing river: Research lessons and the improvement of Japanese education. *American Educator*, pp. 14–17, 50–52.

Rogoff, B. (1995). Observing sociocultural activity on three planes: Participatory appropriation, guided participation, and apprenticeship. In J. V. Wertsch, P. Del Río, & A. Alvarez (Eds.), *Sociocultural studies of mind* (pp. 139–164). New York: Cambridge University Press.

Wenger, E. (1998). *Communities of practice: Learning, meaning, and identity.* New York: Cambridge University Press.

7

Learning to
See the Invisible

Power, Authority, and Language in the Classroom

Tomás Galguera

TG:	Good afternoon.
Students:	Good afternoon.
TG:	Today we're going to focus on one of the "big ideas" in this course, that language is both symbolic of and instrumental for power relations in society. But before we do that, I want to know how many of you read the Ruiz[1] article.

[Most students raise their hands, a few tentatively.]

AUTHOR'S NOTE: All the names used in this chapter are pseudonyms. Excerpts reprinted with permission.

TG: Good! So, who can tell me what the article is about? What's
           Ruiz's main argument?

[After a second or two, a handful of hands go up. The instructor surveys
the room and, after a few seconds, points to Jennifer.]

TG: Jennifer. What can you tell me about Ruiz's article?

Jennifer: That there are problems with the word *empowerment*, at
           least how it is commonly used. I think that Ruiz is saying
           that empowerment means that those in power give a little
           power to those who don't have it, but that doesn't change
           things much. They're still in power.

TG: Yes! Nicely put. There are indeed problems with *empower-
           ment*. Does he propose another term?

[Jennifer shrugs and smiles apologetically, shaking her head.]

TG: Who can tell me? Is there another term that Ruiz proposes
           we use instead of *empowerment* to describe our work with
           English learners?

[After a short period, the instructor calls on Melissa, who does not have
her hand up but is looking at him. She looks around and mouths,
"Me?" pointing at herself before answering.]

Melissa: No, he doesn't. In fact he ends his article inviting others to
           come up with such a term.

TG: Excellent!

[Melissa looks away, looking slightly uncomfortable.]

TG: What else does Ruiz object to? Anyone else?

[The group of students remains quiet, although quite a few have taken
out their readers and have found Ruiz's article. They seem to be
going over their notes, rereading sections, or perhaps reading the
article for the first time. The number of raised hands is still less than
10, their owners look at the instructor, some confidently, others slightly
apprehensively.]

TG: Eric?

Eric: He says that language and voice aren't the same thing and that the goal of schools should be to develop students' voices, not just language.

TG: Good! Is the distinction between these two concepts clear to all? This is important.

[A majority of the students nod. The instructor remains silent, smiling. It takes some time for students to realize that the pause is extending beyond their expectations. They begin looking at each other, a few make quizzical gestures and whisper questions and comments to someone near them.]

TG: So what was going on here? Did you notice anything unusual?

[The group reacts to the instructor's questions with a mixture of mild annoyance, curiosity, and relief. A few students venture comments and questions aloud. Many students shift around in their seats, communicating with others using gestures. Others simply look at the instructor, expectantly. He waits for the reaction to subside, smiling, while leaning on the desk at the front of the room.]

This is the beginning of a class meeting in the "Methodology of English Language Development and Content Instruction" course, during which preservice teachers and I discussed the political nature of teaching in the context of a classroom with English learners.[2] In departing from the norm and using a teacher-centered, didactic approach, I wanted to provide our preservice teachers with a vivid example of classroom discourse as a way to explore its normative and symbolic nature. Much of our work in preparing teachers to teach culturally and linguistically diverse students and students whose own culture and language are different from that of most teachers consists of awakening and developing their awareness toward language and culture. Thus, we rely on a number of activities, exercises, and tasks that allow them to analyze concrete and tangible aspects of culture and language. The staged beginning of this class meeting was followed by a discussion analyzing the discourse and commenting on its educational implications. This was followed by a written response to a prompt and a guided viewing and analysis of a video recording of classroom teaching, all focused on the political nature of teaching and language, and of classroom discourse in particular. In this chapter, we discuss the multilayered political nature of teaching, focusing on language and classroom discourse. Our focus follows our realization that to teach in ways that take into account the political nature of teaching you need to consider both explicit and implicit consequences of your practice, especially the nature of classroom discourse. This is true for future teachers of minority[3] students and of language-minority students in particular, a likely prospect for most preservice teachers in the United States. Thus, we ask you to consider the political implications of the language you and your students use in the classroom, as well as the oral and written language in the content that you teach and the language used within the school community and society at large. As a first step, we examine the literature for useful perspectives on the political nature of teaching. While reading this review and throughout the chapter, we invite you to ask yourself what comes to mind when you think about the political dimensions of teaching. Have you stopped to consider that by its very nature, teaching assumes differences in power, status, and authority between you and your students and among your students? We also discuss pedagogical tools that we use to both assess and foster political awareness among preservice teachers. Think about the power structures that the curriculum and pedagogy you use not only represent but also sustain. We close the chapter with a discussion of the political implications of our work as teachers and teacher educators concerned with social equity and justice. If the goal of schools and education is to provide students with the means to equitably contribute to the democratic process and to the creation of culture, do we subvert systems and practices that limit participation and foster those that enhance it? This is an especially important question for all of us to consider at a time when narrowly defined outcome measures pose serious and lasting consequences for our actions.

❖   HOW IS TEACHING POLITICAL?

Power and authority are inextricably linked to teaching and schooling. Assuming that the desirable outcome of education and teaching is learning, there is much truth to Francis Bacon's assertion that knowledge is power. The nature of this power can be instrumental and enhance our ability to control the physical environment and make our existence more predictable and manageable. This power should be clear to anyone who, by applying mathematical skills learned in school, avoids running out of gas while traversing a particularly desolate section during a road trip. Similarly, as a species, we have achieved significant gains in our quality of life because of research that has built on previous research by fellow humans. Yet, the power we enjoy through our knowledge about the environment and material aspects of our lives comes to us indirectly. For example, we do not have to know much about computers and programming to take advantage of the formidable power that digital technology affords us.

Besides the ability to manipulate the environment to our advantage, either directly or indirectly, knowledge also translates into power over other people. We all have to depend on experts from time to time to help us deal with problems that we encounter in our daily lives. Sometimes their help is altruistic, and sometimes we must compensate them for it, but they always have power over us: Their decision to help us or not will have more or less serious consequences on our quality of life. Thus, the more you know, the greater the power you can exert over others, especially when this expertise is about subjects that have direct and drastic consequences on other people's lives.

With knowledge and power over others comes authority, which is why elders usually exercise authority over youth. This is particularly true in traditional societies, in which elders often made decisions that had significant and lasting impact on the community. Elders were also the first teachers who passed on histories, traditions, values, skills, and norms to new generations. Similarly, individuals who, because of luck or perseverance, gained expertise in a field of knowledge, such as art, literature, medicine, or religion, were often designated as teachers of the new generations, particularly of youth who were deemed fit as future influential and sometimes powerful authority figures (see Emile Durkheim in Giddens, 1972, pp. 203–218). As societies grew and became increasingly complex, who learned what and who taught it became important factors in how power was wielded and shared by different sectors of the population. For instance, in most societies, men exercise a greater share of power than women. As a way to maintain this control, girls have limited access to education. Yet, women predominantly are given the responsibility to educate children, both at home and as teachers. Miller (1996) sees this as the reason why many societies, including our own, frequently talk out of both sides of their mouths regarding teaching: It is deemed critical in determining the fate of future generations *and* often remains a low-status profession.

Ultimately, the reason why teaching is political rests in the fact that in the United States as well as most industrialized countries, knowledge codified in terms of educational attainment remains the single legitimate criterion of discrimination. Although it is generally illegal to discriminate on the basis of race, ethnicity, religion, gender, age, and sexual orientation in these countries, individuals may be denied jobs, group memberships, and social status solely on the basis of their schooling and educational attainment without legal repercussions. Furthermore, we usually see the reasons for such discriminatory practices as self-evident; people need to be adequately trained to perform the tasks associated with a particular job. Because of technological advances, schools must prepare tomorrow's citizens with the necessary skills to be productive. As a result, increasingly greater proportions of the population end up spending increasingly longer periods in school to gain access to better standards of living. This is what sociologists such as Burton Clark (1962) and others have termed a "functional" theory explaining the importance of education in modern society.

A different explanation of the important role that schools play in providing access to power to different individuals and groups is a conflict theory of stratification (Weber, 1968). This theory sees the role of schools not as preparing productive citizens but rather as teaching the culture that is shared by those in power. Educational attainment, particularly at elite schools and universities, is considered synonymous with learning the norms, values, beliefs, and practices of those in power, rather than the technical knowledge and skills we may need for any given job. Just as with functional views, most of us have no problem understanding and justifying the need for students to become proficient in the culture of power. We all hope that others perceive us, and especially our children, as smart and educated individuals, which often translates to being proficient in Standard English, acting "sophisticated," and valuing entrepreneurship, hard work, autonomy, and ambition, among other things.

Clearly, there are elements from both theories that help us understand why educational attainment has become increasingly important in determining the average annual earnings and, by implication, the standard of living of U.S. citizens (National Center for Education Statistics, 2003). Moreover, Americans have traditionally viewed education as the solution to a host of social problems. The real and imagined power of education to change the future of individuals and society has contributed to make it an arena for political struggle, particularly for school reform. In *Tinkering Toward Utopia,* David Tyack and Larry Cuban (1997) describe this process as follows:

> Educational reforms are intrinsically political in origin. Groups organize and contest with other groups in the politics of education to express their values and to secure their interests in the public school. Conflicts in education have arisen over ethnic, religious, racial, gender, and class differences. Controversies over language policies—English only or bilingual instruction—have recurred for over a century, as did contests over racial or gender segregation or the use of the Bible and prayer in schools. (p. 8)

There is no doubt that multiple political interests constantly tug at schools and other educational institutions, especially during election times. Yet, you might argue that once you close your classroom door, all that stays out. You would not be alone. Public education in the United States, either by tacit agreement or by law, has strived to become an institution that is "above politics" and separate from religion (Tyack, 1986, p. 10). These values still resonate with most Americans. However, you do not have to be the proverbial anthropologist from Mars to notice that a power structure indeed defines your behavior and that of your students, even if you are experiencing "discipline" and "classroom management" problems.

In writing about social control, Dewey (1938/1997) compares a classroom situation with that of most cooperative games that children play. He observes that rules controlling individual actions do not violate freedom. Rather, they are necessary for the game to go on. When conflicts or problems arise, either a leader among the children or a parent or other adult exercises authority, but only as a representative of the group. In classrooms, especially those in which few opportunities for meaningful and authentic collaboration exist, the authority of the teacher depends on the students' obedience. In contrast with such an autocratic situation, Dewey believes that, "When education is based upon experience and educative experience is seen to be a social process, the situation changes radically. The teacher loses the position of external boss or dictator but takes on that of leader of group activities" (p. 59).

❖ CRITICAL PEDAGOGY AND
    TEACHERS OF ENGLISH LEARNERS

Whether as group leaders or "external bosses," we *are* authority figures in classrooms, displaying a power differential that is the focus of attention for proponents of critical pedagogy. As with other critical theories, critical pedagogy views teaching practice from an explicitly political perspective, asking who benefits and who suffers from how knowledge is produced and distributed. Its goal is education that is emancipatory. In the words of Henry Giroux (1994), one of its most salient proponents, "Pedagogy in the critical sense illuminates the relationship among knowledge, authority, and power" (p. 30).

Paolo Freire (1972), another well-known thinker associated with critical pedagogy, rejects the notion of teachers as knowers and students as empty vessels in which to deposit this knowledge, a "banking" model of teaching. Instead, he insists on the need for equity in the status of teachers "so that both are simultaneously teachers and students" (p. 59). Freire insists that the relationship between teacher and students must be dialectical in order for true knowledge to be constructed. In his words, "True dialogue unites subjects together in the cognition of a knowable object which mediates between them" (Freire, 1970, p. 253).

After our discussion about the ways in which teaching is political and this all-too-brief introduction to a few basic critical pedagogy notions, you may be asking yourself, how does all this relate to how I teach? In analyzing the political nature of teaching, we run the risk of getting lost in layer upon layer of implications, concerns, and possibilities. A comprehensive examination of such complexity would require much more space than this chapter. Instead, we invite you to examine the political nature of classroom discourse as one of several ways in which teaching is political. By making the invisible visible, you will gain a deeper appreciation of the symbolic and instrumental functions of English as the language of power, a necessary perspective when you teach English learners. We cannot say that this is an easy process; nor can we promise you easy, practical solutions. Yet, a critical awareness of classroom discourse will provide you with a vantage point for the examination of knowledge, authority, and power, and it has direct implications for your teaching practice.

In the case of teachers of English learners, English is the obvious "knowable object" (Freire, 1970, p. 253) around which a dialectical relationship may be built. Although enhanced consciousness is but the first step toward emancipation and, thus, greater equity, it is difficult to achieve. At first, it may not seem necessary for teachers, who presumably are proficient in English, to know English. However, humans' natural ability to interpret and produce appropriate forms in any given language depends primarily on the content of such forms, especially after achieving a minimum level of fluency. In using language, we do not need to attend to every surface nuance in either language production or interpretation. Doing so would tax our conscious mind beyond capacity and would seriously limit our capacity to communicate. As Leo Van Lier (1995) writes, "Language is as important to human beings as water is to fish. Yet, it often seems that we go through life as unaware of language as we suppose the average fish is of the water it swims in" (p. xi). In line with the notion of raising awareness toward language are ways of teaching that lead to Freire's (1972) notion of *concientization* (p. 81), or the raising of teachers' and students' critical consciousness of themselves and their place in the world.

❖ CRITICAL LANGUAGE AWARENESS

However radical and revolutionary critical pedagogy principles may seem, especially when they first appeared in the educational research community, critics have found faults with the inaccessible language used by its proponents and with its apparent lack of usefulness for everyday classroom practice (Ellsworth, 1989; Johnston, 1999). Sensitive to this criticism, we turn to Norman Fairclough (1989), who proposes studying discourse for "a theory of social action—social practice—which accounts for both the determining effect of conventions and the strategic creativity of social speakers, without reducing practice to one or the other" (p. 10). In other words, Fairclough proposes that we look at our daily use of language (English) to better understand how we all are shaped and influenced by it while we continue to use it and learn about it in creative ways.

Fairclough (1989) thinks critical language awareness is developed through increased consciousness among teachers and students about how language contributes to create and sustain inequity among humans. He believes that such consciousness is a critical prerequisite to achieve greater social equity and justice. The goal of developing critical language awareness in you, and especially among English learners in your classroom, is more than just developing linguistic, grammatical, or communicative competencies. Rather, critical language awareness and, ultimately, emancipatory discourse is about realizing that "language use—discourse—is not just a matter of performing tasks, it is also a matter of expressing and constituting and reproducing social identities and social relations, including crucially relations of power" (Fairclough, 1989, p. 237). Fairclough proposes that we all engage in *critical language study* (CLS) as a method to achieve the critical language awareness he sees as essential for teachers and students of language.

Greater consciousness (i.e., *concientization;* Freire, 1970) by itself does not always lead to greater participation in power structures by previously marginalized groups and individuals. Likewise, favorable conditions must exist for CLS to result in more democratic participation in education and, eventually, society. On the one hand, language minority groups must be ready, willing, and able to recognize their lack of privilege; they can do this only through their own experience. On the other hand, teachers as agents of change must have both the necessary theoretical background and enough shared experience with students to be accepted as such. Besides these two subjective conditions, objective conditions that allow social emancipation among language learners must also exist. The latter may be either institutional or sociopolitical and are applicable to various levels of education and society (Fairclough, 1989, p. 234).

Fairclough (1989) proposes a CLS model that rests on two principles: (a) critical language awareness should occur concurrently with purposeful discourse practice and (b) critical language awareness should emanate from individuals' own experiences and linguistic capabilities. Fairclough also conceives the development of critical language awareness on two levels: First, language learners must realize the wealth of resources they possess to participate in discourse; typically, language learners are not aware of these resources. This process requires explicit understanding of language as a symbolic system. Also, according to the practice principle described above, awareness is best developed through analysis of language learners' own discourse. In turn, awareness leads to growth in discourse participation capabilities. Second, once language learners understand the manner in which they participate in discourse, they can begin to explain the influence that social and political forces have on discourse and the manner in which discourse reflects and changes social relations and relations of power. According to the practice principle, consciousness about the sociopolitical determinants of discourse and the effects of one's own discourse will result in emancipatory discourse. Furthermore, the experience principle suggests that language learners should be taught explicitly a language model and a metalanguage that enables them to reflect and talk about their own language experiences and abilities (pp. 240–241).

❖ CRITICAL LANGUAGE AWARENESS DEVELOPMENT TOOLS

The demonstration with which we began this chapter is but one way to make explicit the need for teachers to develop critical language awareness. Consonant with critical pedagogy and CLS, the goal behind this exercise is for you and other preservice teachers to understand that teaching is indeed political in its various layers and contexts and to help you develop a consonant teaching practice. We must all strive to become teachers who understand how teaching, schools, and education as a whole are and can be political and politicized. We must also become agents of change in the realm of local, state, and federal laws and policies that impact schools, our teaching practice, and the fate of our students, especially of historically disadvantaged students. We hope that reading this and the other chapters in this book will help you understand the often invisible ways in which classroom discourse is both instrumental for and symbolic of power relations in society.

We now present a set of tasks and exercises that can help you develop what Freire (Freire & Macedo, 1987) calls "political clarity," or the ability to "[transcend] the perception of life as a pure biological process to arrive at a perception of life as a biographical, historical, and collective process" (p. 130). Our hope is not only that you, as present or future teachers of disempowered students, will prepare future citizens with power to change the world for the better but that you will also gain in your ability to change the world as a "transformative intellectual" (Giroux, 1987, p. 25).

One set of tools consists of language awareness demonstrations (such as the one presented at the beginning of this chapter), simulations, and other similar experiences, which are followed by individual reflective analysis and both small-group and whole-class discussions on the practical implications of the insights gained from these procedures. Another set of tools consists of classroom discourse analysis tasks and exercises designed with the intention of enhancing language awareness as well as providing you with authentic opportunities to develop a metalanguage. In addition to these experiences, preservice teachers experience, as students, examples of pedagogy that are appropriate for English learners at different levels of proficiency and grade levels. We follow these hands-on examples with a critical analysis of the theoretical and empirical reasons behind them, emphasizing the political subtext in them. These tools, together, are intended to help preservice teachers (a) understand the relationship between classroom discourse and power and status; (b) become articulate and proficient in discussing the political nature of teaching and, particularly, of classroom discourse; and (c) understand their own power and responsibility to change their classrooms, education, and the world through their own teaching and other professional and personal dimensions. Let us now turn to an analysis and discussion of examples of each one of these tools. As you read through each of these examples, try to think about the issues raised that relate to your own experiences and thoughts about how language and classroom discourse relate to power and status. Consider other ways in which teaching is indeed political.

Language Awareness Exercises

During the discussion that followed the demonstration that opens this chapter, the preservice teachers described feeling somewhat surprised by the manner in which the class had begun, but none felt the change was serious enough to merit asking or commenting about it in front of everyone. Laughing, Lisa, one of the preservice teachers, confessed thinking that perhaps the instructor was "mad at them for something," which explained why he "was being mean." Jamie talked about suspecting that the instructor "was up to something," which was why she had not "played along" by raising her hand to answer what were obviously display questions (Long & Sato, 1983). However, when asked whether they thought the instructor's teaching was inappropriate, they all answered no. Rebecca said that she had thought "this style of teaching stinks," but that it was a way of teaching she had experienced before. This comment was received with widespread laughter.

When asked whether they had noticed any patterns in the language used during the demonstration, the question was received mostly with puzzled looks, and a few asked "What do you mean?" We all use language in predictable ways, and turn-taking is one of the fundamental and predictable patterns of language use. What could they say about turn-taking during the exchanges in this demonstration? What do *you* notice? Who started the exchanges? Who ended them? What was said during each turn? These preservice teachers observed that I, as the instructor, mostly had asked questions and then told them whether their answers were right or wrong. This is a common pattern in most classrooms, one that is well known among researchers of English as a Second Language (ESL) classrooms: question-response-evaluation (Edwards & Westgate, 1994) and question-response-feedback (Simich, 1984; Simich-Dudgeon, McCreedy, & Schleppegrell, 1988; Tharp & Gallimore, 1991). Having experienced it, and then having that experience made explicit through whole-group discussion, made the power relations inherent in such a discussion much clearer. I then asked our preservice teachers to discuss in small groups what implications such discourse patterns had for students and the nature of knowledge and learning and to report a summary of their discussions afterward.

Most of the small-group reports referred to the fact that discourse patterns such as these were not limited to ESL classrooms. The preservice teachers observed that question-response-evaluation/feedback patterns conveyed a notion of right-and-wrong knowledge, with teachers as the ultimate knowers and authority figures. Can you see how this seemingly innocuous classroom practice is indeed a powerful marker of power relations in most classrooms? The large-group discussion also touched on the fact that, rather than a dialogue, the resulting exchange worked, minimally, as a way to assess and evaluate the diligence and ability of a few students. One thing was clear: My statements were the dominant voice, with students' contributions sounding mostly tentative and minimal. In this case, the teacher is the expert, the knower; a message that is often magnified by curricula and evaluations that exclude the students' perspectives, effectively silencing their voices. This experience and discussion served to highlight the contrast between authentic and display questions and the relative predominance of the latter over the former in most classrooms. This is an especially important point to consider when teaching students who need ample opportunities to practice using academic English (Valdés, 2001), not simply to answer closed-ended questions. We mulled over possible consequences of reversing this pattern and considered ways of doing so. The preservice teachers acknowledged that occasionally, it may be necessary for teachers to use question-response-evaluation/feedback patterns to assert their authority, which raised the question of professional judgment and decision making in teaching (Shulman, 2002).

Another exercise intended to develop both metalinguistic and metacognitive awareness consists of asking preservice teachers to play the role of students in a lesson taught entirely in Spanish and to complete related work in Spanish[4] as well. Have you ever experienced being taught academic content in a second language? What might be some of the feelings and thoughts that you would experience? What is the relationship between knowledge, power, and authority in such a situation? Consider these questions as you read the next paragraph.

I began the class by explaining, in English, that I would be teaching in Spanish, asking students to notice their feelings and thoughts throughout. At the end of the simulation, they would be expected to write about it. After making sure that they understood the task, I switched to Spanish and did not speak English again until the end of the lesson, which lasted about 15 minutes in all. The lesson in Spanish began with the question, Did you know that California is notorious because of its frequent earthquakes? I modeled the use of *sí* and *no* to answer and wrote words such as *terremotos* (earthquakes), *fallas* (faults), and *sismógrafo* (seismograph) on the board, acting out their meanings. I described my own experiences during the 1989 Loma Prieta earthquake, frequently gesturing and exaggerating intonations as well as writing down on the board words that described my feelings. Next, I asked the preservice teachers to choose from another list of words on the board that described where they might have been when this earthquake hit (e.g., *en mi casa, en el trabajo, en mi carro,* etc.). I then handed out a paper with several questions and spent time not only going over these but also asking students for strategies they might use in answering them. Finally, I handed out earthquake preparedness brochures published in Spanish by the U.S. Geological Survey. I modeled looking at the title and venturing guesses about the content and spent time talking about the illustrations and headings before asking students to complete the handout individually first and as a group later. After allowing students to work for a few minutes, I switched again to English, announcing the end of the simulation.

The preservice teachers then completed a quickwrite responding to the following prompts: What were your thoughts, feelings, and/or "gut reaction" to what you just experienced? What things did you notice about teaching and learning from this? What concepts, ideas, models, or theories come to mind that can help you understand this experience? Their writing and the discussion that followed revealed a range of responses, from success and elation at understanding "almost everything" to frustration and disappointment for understanding "very little." The three students who were quite proficient in Spanish wrote about feeling privileged and even slightly "guilty." Many commented on how this experience provided them with an opportunity to share the experience of the English learners in English-only classrooms, a common situation in California since the passage of Proposition 227, the voters' initiative that effectively outlawed bilingual instruction in the state. Some felt relieved to find out that other people in their groups had also struggled with the task and were appreciative of the knowledge that others brought to the task. They wished they could answer the questions in English instead of Spanish, as they had been required to do. They also noticed what was useful for them; specifically, background knowledge, including the use of familiar words (e.g., Loma Prieta), and listing on the board and explaining additional vocabulary words. Kim felt challenged to the point of frustration and reflected on the situation in which many English learners find themselves. She wondered whether she, as an English learner, might choose to persevere and learn English or disengage.

> I know almost no Spanish, so I was lost on what was going on most of the time. I still paid attention to see if I could get an idea of what you were talking about—which is where your movement, repetition of certain words, and usage of words I understood (e.g., California) really helped. I did feel alienated from the rest of the class because I had no clue [about] what you were asking—yet quite a few people responded (which I didn't understand either). The words on the board helped me gain a little clarity, as seeing words helps me decipher them, and many Spanish and English words look alike.
>
> With the rest of the lesson, I continued to feel lost, although I was able to answer [questions] 1 and 2 by slowly deciphering the question and looking in the book for the same words as in the questions. I guess the way I feel [this] is the same way a student would feel in a class where they did not understand the language. It would be full immersion—like many kids are forced to undertake at school. I suppose if I had to be in this kind of environment day after day, I might eventually learn Spanish, but I would get so frustrated along the way that I might not hang in there long enough.

Andrea, on the other hand, found the experience "enjoyable" and appreciated the challenge of drawing meaning both from my words and the text. However, she recognizes that this was "only an experiment" and as such, the stakes were low. She expresses a deep concern for English learners' daily experiences and the cost that such experiences might have for their self-esteem and sense of self-efficacy. The second part of her reflection suggests that this exercise provided her with a valuable perspective on her own perspectives and high self-expectations as a literate person.

> Listening to your Spanish lecture was actually enjoyable. It was nice to be able to latch onto a few key words that helped me understand the topic (Earthquakes & the Bay Area). I recognize that being fully aware of the fact that your Spanish lecture was "only an experiment" gave me some comfort and allowed me to go with the flow. Deep in my heart, though, I felt anguish and pain as I only momentarily got a glimpse of what many students experience on a daily basis. For those students who struggle to understand their teacher's instructions, being able to "pick out key words" isn't entertaining and enjoying. . . . It isn't enough to help them feel confident and competent.
>
> The writing portion of the assignment brought out interesting [and] complex feelings within me. I was able to locate the "answers" to your questions, but I was frustrated because I could not answer (your Spanish questions) in complete sentences. Part of being a high-achieving, literate person means (for me) that you can write in complete sentences. And I felt frustrated as I imagine bright English learners feel.

The preservice teachers' responses to these exercises clearly suggest that they are beginning to gain an awareness regarding important elements of diversity among their students as well as language use and language acquisition. It remains to be seen whether this awareness influences their teaching practice. As others have noted (e.g., Ellsworth, 1989; Johnston, 1999), it is indeed difficult to translate critical theories in general and critical pedagogy in particular into practical teaching applications. Some of this may be due to the overly theoretical nature of the content in most teacher-education programs (Korthagen & Kessels, 1999). A more likely reason for this may lie in the very complex nature of the work and the numerous dilemmas that surface as one gains political clarity (Freire & Macedo, 1987).

❖ THE DILEMMA OF REPRESENTATION
AND PARTICIPATION

One of the outcomes of raising the awareness among students about issues of representation, access, and power in the context of classrooms with language minority students is the recognition of a dilemma: How is it possible to recognize, legitimize, and value the students' particular language varieties meaningfully and simultaneously teach them the language of power? This dilemma of representation and participation in education among English learners is particularly troublesome when the students in question come from marginalized backgrounds, when xenophobic attitudes dominate the public discourse, *and* when their teachers have little in common with them. By emphasizing the students' end of this opposition and thus making their particular language variations not only a valid voice in the classroom but also a worthy subject of study, teachers are likely to face stiff opposition.

Dominant groups in society see attempts to democratize education at best as wasteful utilization of resources and at worst as threats to education as an institution. Moreover, in what may seem contradictory at first, English learners, who are predominantly marginalized inside and outside of school, are also likely to view with suspicion any attempts by teachers to validate and study non-high-status English forms. Perhaps nothing illustrates better this opposition to progressive, critical pedagogy than the appearance of Proposition 227, a ballot initiative that proposed to do away with bilingual education programs at once. Among its supporters were found not only those representing mainstream interests but also the parents of English learners, who are most likely to benefit from bilingual instruction.

Even under favorable circumstances, teachers of English learners must still come to terms with the fact that by recognizing and teaching preferred discourse patterns (i.e., Standard English), they in fact reinforce and sustain the status quo. Attempts to explore non-Standard English variations in the classroom become nothing more than window dressing and excursions into exotic forbidden territory instead of a democratic exercise in education. Rather than expanding the range of expression, these nominal attempts at diversifying classroom discourse often have the opposite effect. They provide an opportunity to contrast preferred and marginalized discourse norms, caricaturing the latter.

The dilemma as stated above is a facet of the larger tension surrounding public education as one of the engines driving the construction of culture. From a traditional, conservative perspective, the charter of public education must be the upholding of social and cultural norms. This position assumes that these norms are relatively static and easily captured in content to be taught to receptive students. Implicit in this perspective is the view of teachers as public employees hired to carry out the will of the citizens and not to advance subversive agendas, regardless of how progressive these agendas may be. In this sense, attempts by teachers to promote critical thinking among their students may be construed as a breach of contract between public school teachers and the public, especially when such thinking leads to students' questioning existing power and values systems.

You, as a beginning or experienced teacher, are likely to face similar dilemmas and questions regarding the nature of knowledge, power, and authority in your classroom. Careful consideration of these issues is likely to make you a better teacher, ideally one with political clarity (Freire & Macedo, 1987). As such, you will soon realize that the political nature of teaching is itself embedded in a larger power structure in which teachers lack the authority and power to define not only their own profession but even what and how they teach. We encourage you to work toward developing a critical awareness of classroom discourse, as well as of curriculum, materials, evaluations and assessments, pedagogy, and work to ensure that your students' voices join a democratic chorus. Yet, how do you understand the power structure that governs schools and, by implication, defines much of your daily work? What are ways in which you and other teachers can influence decisions and policies that are likely to have lasting—although not always desirable—consequences for you and your students? We chose to discuss the political nature of teaching by focusing on classroom discourse precisely because of its invisibility. However, we do not ignore the more overt political dimensions of teaching. Far from it, political clarity (Freire & Macedo, 1987) cannot be kept captive inside yours or anyone's classroom.

❖ CONCLUSION

We began this chapter with a transcript from a demonstration, and, throughout the rest of the chapter, we described tools we use to support the development of teachers who understand the personal, professional, and societal implications associated with thinking of teaching as a political act. Yet, we realize that the same is true of our situation as educators. We cannot escape the fact that our role as teacher educators, down to the very pedagogy and materials we use, carries with it political dimensions that are not always apparent but constantly and pervasively influence our practice and our view of the world. I decided to use this demonstration to achieve certain goals, even if this implied a certain abuse of the authority that students, the university, and society as a whole had given me. However, I am also required to meet standards and expectations that fellow faculty, both inside and outside my department, believe necessary for themselves as professionals. Furthermore, the California Standards for the Teaching Profession further constrain and define our practice. It is within this multilayered spider web of power and authority that we all must learn to function, but especially the future teachers of children who increasingly are trapped at the bottom layers of even greater webs. Our task is often made the more difficult by conflicting interests, themselves the result of, at best, ill-conceived and, at worst, ill-intended laws, policies, and practices. Similar to the dilemma of representation and participation in education we discuss above, educators must face countless decisions with cascading political implications. We believe that each one of us will do what is best for our students and for ourselves as teachers, a difficult balance to achieve indeed, but a task for which we need as much political clarity (Freire & Macedo, 1987) as possible.

❖ NOTES

1. The chapter the students had read was Ruiz (1997).

2. In California schools, 44% of all K through 3 students and more than 25% of students in all grades have been designated "English learners," or "students for whom there is a report of a primary language other than English on the state-approved *Home Language Survey and* [their emphasis] who, on the basis of the state-approved oral language (grades K-12) assessment procedures and including literacy (grades 3–12 only), have been determined to lack the clearly defined English language skills of listening comprehension, speaking, reading, and writing necessary to succeed in the school's regular instructional programs" (California Department of Education, 2003).

3. Our use of the term *minority* is to describe the sociopolitical status of linguistic, ethnic, racial, and cultural groups, not their proportional ranking in the population.

4. Although a few of our students are somewhat proficient in Spanish, most either do not speak it at all or speak it at an early beginning proficiency level.

❖ REFERENCES

California Department of Education. (2003). *Number of English learners in California public schools, by language and grade ranked by total, 2002–03, statewide.* http://data1.cde.ca.gov.

Clark, B. R. (1962). *Educating the expert society.* San Francisco: Chandler.

Dewey, J. (1997). *Experience and education.* New York: Touchstone. (Original work published 1938)

Edwards, A. D., & Westgate, D. P. G. (1994). *Investigating classroom talk* (2nd ed.). London: Falmer.

Ellsworth, E. (1989). Why doesn't this feel empowering? Working through the repressive myths of critical pedagogy. *Harvard Educational Review, 59* (3), 297–324.

Fairclough, N. (1989). *Language and power.* London: Longman.

Freire, P. (1970). The adult literacy process as cultural action for freedom. *Harvard Educational Review, 40,* 205–225.

Freire, P. (1972). *Pedagogy of the oppressed.* New York: Seabury.

Freire, P., & Macedo, D. (1987). *Literacy: Reading the word and the world.* Westport, CT: Bergin & Garvey.

Giddens, A. (Ed.). (1972). *Emile Durkheim: Selected writings.* New York: Cambridge University Press.

Giroux, H. A. (1987). Introduction. In P. Freire & D. Macedo, *Literacy: Reading the word and the world* (pp. 1–27). Westport, CT: Bergin & Garvey.

Giroux, H. A. (1994). *Disturbing pleasures: Learning popular culture.* New York: Routledge.

Johnston, B. (1999). Putting critical pedagogy in its place: A critical account. *TESOL Quarterly, 33* (3), 557–565.

Korthagen, F. A. J., & Kessels, J. P. A. M. (1999). Linking theory and practice: Changing the pedagogy of teacher education. *Educational Researcher, 28* (4), 4–17.

Long, M. H., & Sato, C. J. (1983). Classroom foreigner talk discourse: Forms and functions of teachers' questions. In H. W. Seliger & M. H. Long (Eds.), *Classroom-oriented research in second language acquisition* (pp. 268–286). Rowley, MA: Newbury House.

Miller, J. (1996). *School for women.* London: Virago.

National Center for Education Statistics (2003). Annual earnings: Difference in average annual earnings (in constant 2000 dollars) for all wage and salary workers ages 25–34 between the highest and lowest quartiles, by sex and educational attainment: March 1971–2000. http://nces.ed.gov/programs/coe/2002/charts/chart16b.asp

Ruiz, R. (1997). The empowerment of language-minority students. In A. Darder, R. D. Torres, & H. Gutiérrez (Eds.) *Latinos and education: A critical reader.* New York: Routledge.

Shulman, L. S. (2002). Making differences: A table of learning. *Change, 34* (6), 36–44.

Simich, C. (1984). *A sociolinguistic investigation of the structure of sixth grade science and arts lessons with particular attention to verification of learning activities.* Unpublished doctoral dissertation, Georgetown University.

Simich-Dudgeon, C., McCreedy, L., & Schleppegrell, M. J. (1988). *Helping limited English proficient children communicate in the classroom: A handbook for teachers.* Washington, DC: The Center for Applied Linguistics.

Tharp, R. G., & Gallimore, R. (1991). *The instructional conversation: Teaching and learning in social activity.* Santa Cruz, CA: The National Center for Research on Cultural Diversity and Second Language Learning.

Tyack, D. B. (1986). *Managers of virtue: Public school leadership in America, 1820–1980.* New York: Basic Books.

Tyack, D. B., & Cuban, L. (1997). *Tinkering toward utopia: A century of public school reform.* Cambridge, MA: Harvard University Press.

Valdés, G. (2001). *Learning and not learning English: Latino students in American schools.* New York: Teachers College Press.

Van Lier, L. (1995). *Introducing language awareness.* London: Penguin English.

Weber, M. (1968). *Economy and society: An outline of interpretive sociology* (G. Roth & C. Wittich, Eds.). New York: Bedminster Press.

8

Principled Practice in a World of Standards

Some Concluding Thoughts

Vicki Kubler LaBoskey

Anna Ershler Richert

Linda R. Kroll

❖ ❖ ❖

The purpose of this text has been to advocate for a principled approach to teaching. We have done so by articulating a set of six principles and describing some possible ways in which they might guide and inform educational practice. Because the whole is always greater than the sum of its parts, we wish to conclude by reviewing and summarizing what we mean by principled practice and the rationale behind it.

❖ WHAT IS PRINCIPLED PRACTICE?

A principled approach to practice begins with the identification and formulation of a set of principles that can guide decisions about how to design and implement educational programs aimed at personal, institutional, and social transformation. The principles need to include, therefore, definitions of teaching and learning and the purpose of each as it is derived from and well justified by empirical and philosophical literature in the field. Individually and collectively, your principles must be consistent with and supportive of your larger goals—which for us includes the compelling goals of social justice, equity, and democracy. The principles need to represent what is currently known about how best to ensure equitable and excellent outcomes for all learners, and they should promote the political and ethical will to pursue these ends.

Once constructed, such a set of principles can inform your decisions about both what to teach and how to teach it. As teachers embrace a set of principles, those principles can provide a vision, a philosophy, and a set of goals toward which the work of teaching can be directed. At the same time, a solid set of principles can operate as guidelines or criteria for developing the means for attaining your goals, for making decisions about curriculum, pedagogy, and even institutional structures. In that sense, the principles can also serve as a set of standards by which to evaluate the consistency of your efforts and the quality of your progress.

A principled approach to teaching is not prescriptive; it is not a list of dos and don'ts. Indeed, quite the opposite is true. A principled approach provides a set of criteria and vision statements that will both encourage and guide educational decision making. It is a system that requires and supports teachers and other educators in making complex professional judgments in both the best and the most challenging of times. Teaching guided by principles allows for a flexible and adaptable approach while at the same time requiring (and assuming) contextual sensitivity and responsiveness. The examples of teaching that we have included in the chapters preceding this are meant to illustrate this adaptive approach. Because change is inevitable, building a teaching practice that is responsive to change is essential. The earlier examples are meant to illustrate how teachers respond to the contextual factors while at the same time holding firm to the goal of excellent outcomes.

Given this inevitability of change, it is important to note that even the principles themselves need to be amenable to change; they should be reconsidered from time to time in light of new research, theoretical development, and more enlightened political and ethical perspectives. We believe principles should not be abandoned, altered, or supplanted arbitrarily or impulsively, however. In principled practice, not just any principle will do. Although we do not presume that the six principles we have provided here are the only ones possible, we do consider them to be empirically and theoretically justified. They continue to be solidly aligned with the goals of equity and justice, which are of primary importance to us. In addition, the principles have been successfully tested in our practice over the last 15 years. For these reasons, we believe they are clearly worthy candidates for consideration in that they can provide new teachers with a solid foundation and promising beginning to their own principled practice.

❖ WHY PRINCIPLED PRACTICE?

Perhaps before accepting these principles as guides for teaching practice, there are questions that warrant prior consideration: Why take a principled approach? What benefit does such an approach offer? To answer these probes, we must return to our opening claim that it is democracy we are after in doing this work. Our aim is to prepare and support teachers who can teach with the goal of contributing to a vibrant, healthy, responsive democracy. But aiming for democracy is not enough. We must teach in democratic ways as well—and help our students and other prospective and experienced teachers do so at the same time. We know that such an approach to education can never be formulaic or regularized. Our reading of the literature that describes and explores democratic education and democracy as an educational aim makes that eminently clear—as does our experience doing this work. Teaching democratically is just as messy, idiosyncratic, cumbersome, and time consuming as political democracy itself. If our aim is to contribute to a healthy democracy characterized by equity and social justice, we can do no less than to practice democracy ourselves in terms of both what we teach and how we do so.

In teaching democratically, we assume that all students are worthy and capable. We hold high expectations for all learners and aim for universally excellent outcomes. Given that no two people are alike—that there is tremendous variation in the needs, interests, styles, languages, skills, understandings, and experiences of our students—the only way in which we can ensure that all will meet those high standards is by flexible and responsive teaching that is context sensitive and culturally relevant. As we have described in the chapters that precede this, teaching is complex work that demands a broad knowledge base, not only of subject matter but of learning theories, instructional methodologies and their theoretical frameworks, cultural and social systems, and particular learners and their contexts. As a teacher, you must be able and willing to make sophisticated and conscientious judgments with regularity that draw on a range of data sources and informational categories. You must be able to provide a variety of means for both enhancing and assessing student understanding. In this conception, *equitable* does not mean sameness. Indeed, equity demands differentiation. Neither democratic teaching nor the means for assessing it can be standardized.

We know that this approach flies in the face of current reform efforts, which stress standardization and standardized measures of success. It is consistent, however, with current calls for high standards and excellent and equitable outcomes for all learners. Standards without standardization is what we are arguing for in this book. The argument we have put forward for a principled approach to teaching practice is based on the expectation that all schools, teachers, and students can and should reach appropriately high, rigorous, and thoughtfully constructed standards of achievement. We are arguing also that meeting those standards does not have to occur—nor can it occur—in the same way for all learners or for all the teachers who teach them.

We find many present attempts to evaluate and improve teaching to be iterative prescriptions that tend to eliminate the complexity and ignore differences among children and the circumstances that frame their lives. Appropriate intervention is less likely when differences are ignored. We have found that standardized (and sometimes scripted) prescriptions tend to exacerbate rather than ameliorate the existing achievement gap and other educational inequities. As an alternative, we offer what we have described as a principled approach to teaching practice. Rather than providing a list of predetermined actions and outcomes, a principled approach provides a road map for responding to the unique while holding firm to high standards for all.

❖ PRINCIPLED PRACTICE AS PROFESSIONAL PRACTICE

The principled approach to teaching that we put forth in this text is a professional orientation to teaching practice. It requires a solid base of knowledge combined with a set of skills and dispositions that direct teachers to determine a course of action and to act as they know best in the interest of the children and communities they serve. Preparing teachers with the knowledge, skills, and dispositions for this august responsibility—and supporting you in doing this work—is what professional education must be about. The inherently uncertain and changing nature of the world in which teachers work suggests that predetermined answers to questions that are not yet known and situations that are yet to occur is foolhardy. Instead, as teachers, you must be prepared with the knowledge, skills, and dispositions to make sense of the circumstances that face you, even as the circumstances change from minute to minute and day to day. As you assess what has happened and what needs to happen next—in line with the goal of excellent outcomes for the children you teach—you are required to make important judgments about how to act (judgments about what to teach and how to teach), then to act, and finally to study the outcomes of those actions in preparation for the next step in the teaching and learning work. This knowledge and set of skills and dispositions are grounded in the principles, which serve as a touchstone against which we can measure our practice.

The principles we have described in this volume provide a foundation for this kind of professional thinking and professional teaching practice. As teachers assume the responsibility that society has placed in their hands to prepare all children with the knowledge and skills they need to chart the course of their lives, to access their share of the riches of this bountiful land, and to participate in creating and sustaining a healthy democracy, they must have as a guide for the work not a set of discrete practices but a well-grounded set of knowledge and beliefs. From this knowledge base, they can generate a course of action that is both appropriate to the circumstances they face and aligned with the goals set by themselves and their learners. We believe that the key to real educational transformation is in the acknowledgment and support of teachers as professionals who must make complex decisions based on significant specialized knowledge appropriate to a particular set of contextual circumstances. We suggest that taking a principled approach to teaching will allow teachers to do just that and, in so doing, will lead us toward the healthy, inclusive democracy that is our goal.

Index